COMMAND THE ROOM

COMMAND THE ROOM

An Essential Guide to the
Purpose, Plan, and Power Behind
Great Speeches and Presentations

GREG SMITH
VINCE BEVACQUA

COPYRIGHT © 2024 GREG SMITH, VINCE BEVACQUA
All rights reserved.

COMMAND THE ROOM
An Essential Guide to the Purpose, Plan, and Power Behind Great Speeches and Presentations

FIRST EDITION

ISBN 978-1-5445-4612-4 *Paperback*
      978-1-5445-4611-7 *Ebook*

CONTENTS

FOREWORD 9
INTRODUCTION 13
PREFACE 19

PART 1: THE PURPOSE
1. WHY DO SPEAKERS NEED PURPOSE? 25
2. WHY DO SPEAKERS NEED VALUES? 29
3. USING ASSESSMENTS TO CLARIFY ONE'S
   PURPOSE AND VALUES 31
4. THE MESSAGE 37
5. MIND YOUR MINDSET 43

PART 2: THE POWER
6. STORY 55
7. PERSONAL STORY 61
8. EMOTIONAL CONTENT 69
9. PRACTICE AND FAIL 77
10. VOICE 83

PART 3: THE PLAN
11. WHAT'S THE PLAN? 97
12. HOW VERSUS WHY 107
13. WORDS, WORDS, WORDS 115
14. MAY I HAVE YOUR ATTENTION, PLEASE? 119
15. THE ASK 123

PART 4: PUTTING IT ALL TOGETHER
16. VOICE CARE AND MAINTENANCE 131
17. MOVEMENT 141
18. VIDEO 153
19. AGAIN, PRACTICE 165
20. STAGE FRIGHT 171

FAREWELL 177
ACKNOWLEDGMENTS 179

FOREWORD

HAVE YOU EVER LISTENED TO A PRESENTATION THAT completely shifted the way you felt or a message that changed your entire perspective or a speech that made you excited to take action? That's the power of impactful communication, the ability to command the room—a skill anyone can acquire and master.

With over two decades in the speaking industry, I have seen countless presentations fall flat. However, I've also experienced the extraordinary power of speeches that captivate and move millions. The most successful communicators possess a unique skill; they profoundly connect with their audience, earning their trust and evoking action, leaving a lasting impression—their words resonating long after the last syllable is spoken.

That's exactly what Greg Smith and Vince Bevacqua will teach you in *Command the Room*.

Not only do they teach it; they exemplify it.

The greatest speakers of our time create influence and impact in every audience. Even though many might just think it's natural talent or charisma that gives them that edge and sets them apart, there are actually certain skills that these leaders use to powerful effect.

Greg Smith is one of those people. He has an ability to connect, communicate, and lead those around him, helping to bring out the best in every person he meets.

I remember the first time I met Greg. Towering over six feet tall, with a booming voice, he had this commanding presence that filled the room, the kind of energy that makes you, and everyone else, take notice. But here's the twist: rather than being intimidating, his smile—in fact, his whole demeanor—radiated warmth and created an immediate connection, like meeting a leader who instantly welcomes you into his inner circle. One interaction with Greg and you know you've encountered someone remarkable.

Having had the honor of working with Greg over the past six years, I have witnessed his generosity and impact as he transforms lives...daily. From his many years of running his own remarkable TEDxYoungstown events and spreading ideas globally to teaching his students at Youngstown State University to speak with confidence and conviction to dramatically up-leveling his clients in vocal training to amplify their messages to leading his entire organization at Compco, Greg creates significant impact through connecting with those he comes in contact with, making them feel seen, heard, and empowered.

When it comes to stellar communication, Greg has a gift. Anytime he steps into a room, his magnetism, confidence, and charisma flow so naturally. Yet I know he has developed, practiced, and refined those skills behind the scenes. Much like any professional athlete makes their ability look like innate talent, they have actually dedicated the time to training, expanding, and taking those skills to the next level.

Greg has done just that, and I'm delighted to see that he is sharing these insights, processes, and techniques with others. In order to effect change in our world, we need powerful speakers who can influence and communicate clearly.

Now Vince is a force in and of himself. With an admirable combination of broadcast journalism and public relations in his tool kit, he has a unique spin on all things communication. As a TV anchor and reporter for over twenty-five years, Vince knows what it takes to earn an audience's attention and, even more importantly, keep it. Only someone who has been reporting in the field for a significant amount of time would understand these skills at such an immersive level. Imagine having only minutes to convey a message that is delicate, dangerous, or even devastating...Vince has done all the above before the first commercial break.

In fact, Vince regularly makes such an impression on his audience he often gets stopped in the grocery store, where people say, "You did such a great job on the news." While Vince hasn't been on the news in fifteen years, he has earned a permanent memory in viewers' minds. *That's* commanding the room, both remote and in person, and with staying power.

Having honed his ability to craft compelling narratives and connect with audiences of all ages over the years, Vince's impact as a trusted source is vast. Adding a focus on public relations and helping business leaders with their many communications challenges has allowed him to expand his influence even further, insights of which he covers in simplified detail in this book as he reveals effective techniques and tactics that are essential for powerful presentations.

Vince's strategic communication skills and story savvy are vital assets for making messaging and public speaking memorable.

What sets this book apart from others is that Greg and Vince don't just talk the talk; they walk the walk.

And with multiple decades of experience behind them, Greg and Vince know how to influence and impact audiences of all sizes.

Generously packed in this book is their vast collective wisdom. What I love about every chapter is that Greg and Vince don't focus on generic theory; they open a treasure chest of actionable strategies reinforced with powerful, relatable stories throughout. Those powerful and memorable stories help the lessons land more significantly. Plus, the pages inside not only address the "how" behind crafting unforgettable speeches and presentations; they also unpack the "why," which is critical for speakers who want to be truly unforgettable.

This book is a must-read for anyone who wants to take their speaking to the next level, who wants to create impact, who wants to be seen...essentially anyone who's ever dreamed of having a voice that captivates a room.

We need great communicators to step into the spotlight and impact change *now*. Our world is waiting to listen.

Kymberlee Weil
Speaking Strategist
Storytelling School LLC
Santa Barbara, California, USA

INTRODUCTION

THE TWO OF US (YOUR AUTHORS) HAVE A SHARED OBSESsion. Something we've both loved our entire lives, though in different settings and for different reasons. We did not know each other as kids, nor did we grow up anywhere near each other. We come from different backgrounds and worked different careers before we met in middle-age and began working together.

Not much in common at all, except for a love of communication.

The very word—"communication"—no longer means what it used to. We've bastardized it in modern American society. "Communication" is now used to house everything from social media posts to couples therapy. And, in our experience, when we force something to include anything, it loses its meaning.

Communication is how humans genuinely connect, build trust, and develop relationships. The medium or mode are secondary concerns. What's important is understanding how we as people add value (whatever that means—love, friendship, education, advocacy) to one another's lives through messaging and how we make that connection more robust, easier, and more effective.

That's the brief explanation. A couple of sentences that summarize decades of passionate work.

For Greg, it all began with his birth. Greg's parents lost their then-only son—Clarence Smith III, known to everyone as Smitty—to a tragic accident; a car struck him while he was playing with his friends. Still grieving for Smitty, Greg's parents brought him into the world. Greg refers to himself as "the replacement child." This would be beyond heartbreaking if the Smiths had withheld feeling from "the replacement." Fortunately, they did not. Loving parents cared for Greg, and his father, Clarence, happily taught Greg about the family businesses.

Back then, Greg's father was involved in several ventures, focusing on metal forming and fabricating. Greg's dad was himself the son of a successful businessman, so by the time Greg came of age to learn, he became the beneficiary of two generations' worth of extraordinary business wisdom.

As Greg became more involved in the family's primary business—Compco, a metal forming company specializing in the production of tank heads—his attention turned more toward the leadership aspects of running a thriving medium-sized company. Greg watched his father listen to his employees, celebrate wins with them, commiserate over losses with them, and manage their day-to-day work. Clarence, known as Mr. Smith, earned the respect and love of Compco's employees. He had a knack for connecting with everyone around him—from the guys on the factory floor to the executives in the C-suite. He was a faithful servant leader who cared about the success and well-being of his employees, and as a result, he managed a staff that stayed on their jobs for years. Parents would encourage their kids to work at Compco. Today, under the fourth generation of Smith family leadership (a milestone that only 2 percent of American companies reach, by the way), other families heavily contribute to the composition of the 150-member team. The workplace is so exceptional it experiences that its staff turnover rate is less than 1 percent.

Surrounded by a great team, Greg could explore leadership as a discipline. He quickly realized that communication is the most critical skill for successful leadership. Leaders are only effective if they can articulate their vision, as well as the plan to achieve it, in clearly understood language.

Always a student who values lifelong learning, Greg sought out teachers and mentors who were nationally and internationally recognized thought leaders. These professionals could inform his growing interest in leadership and communications. Here's a partial roster of people Greg has trained with (and continues to train with today): John Maxwell, Bo Eason, Mary Kincaid, Kymberlee Weil, Jonathan Altfeld, Daniel Teadt, Jack Canfield, and Roger Love. There are others, but you get the idea.

The culmination of all this work and training is Greg's position today: that of a sought-after public-speaking coach. Greg works with business and nonprofit leaders, helping them become the communicators their organizations deserve.

When he is not working with clients or attending to his family's business (he's still Compco's board chairman), Greg teaches communication and public speaking at Youngstown State University. Of all the things that Greg fills his days with, teaching college students is, perhaps, the thing he loves best. In those classrooms, he can enthusiastically share his love of speaking with the leaders of tomorrow.

Vince is the son of a schoolteacher and a social worker. He was a gangly mess growing up—tall and skinny and with more than a few acne blemishes on his face. In high school, he lacked confidence, so while he wanted to engage with his classmates, he wasn't sure how.

Thankfully, his height (Vince is nearly six foot seven today and was close to that by junior high school) attracted the attention of the school's basketball coaches, who took a shy, unathletic young man and patiently mentored him. Vince soon became a captain on the varsity basketball team, and while that was exciting in its own right, the true benefit was that young Vince now had teammates. He had a group of friends he did not have to feel self-conscious around. They supported each other and protected each other.

With this confidence boost, Vince wondered what else he could do. He ran for class president twice and won twice. Now he was in a position where he had to speak to groups of people, and to his surprise, he developed a taste for it. He was unaware then, but someone had planted a seed.

Later, in college, Vince and his roommate started a mobile DJ service. The two played weddings and parties and pretended to be entertainers. Soon, speaking to crowds became familiar…and fun.

Still unsure of what career should follow college, Vince's friends told him, "You like DJing? Why don't you go to graduate school for communications?" The next two years at Emerson College in Boston (the oldest school of communication in the country, by the way), studying broadcast journalism with inspiring professors and enthusiastic fellow students, confirmed this fling with communications was actually true love.

Over the next twenty-five years, Vince would work as a reporter and anchor at TV stations in Massachusetts, Maine, New Hampshire, and Ohio. He would go on to executive positions in PR and marketing firms, open his own boutique PR service helping business leaders with their many communications challenges, and serve briefly as the communications director of a metal forming concern…called Compco.

While at Compco, Greg and Vince collaborated to create a public speaking coaching service that could help any would-be speaker become successful. They poured years of experience—good and bad—into the mix. And the result: a huge pile of content that needed to be sorted, organized, and rendered into something anyone could use to improve their speaking skills.

You are now looking at the result.

We have seen lives change for the better after people learn how to share their vision for the world with others in irresistible ways. There's little you can't do in this world if you can impact how others think and feel using only your message and your voice.

It's not magic (though the results can seem so). Becoming the speaker you aspire to be will take a great amount of focused work and practice. And it can be achieved. You can do it. Guaranteed.

PREFACE

SIXTY-FOUR THOUSAND YEARS AGO, OUR EUROPEAN ancestors painted pictures on cave walls. Most of the images were of prized game animals, and it's believed the paintings were guides to bountiful hunting grounds or perhaps ancient prayers to the gods of nature for successful hunts in the future.

Over fifty-five hundred years ago, the Egyptians spent untold hours carving intricate hieroglyphics into stone, recording major events—such as wars—and honoring their deities.

About six hundred years ago, a German goldsmith named Johannes Gutenberg invented the printing press. Prior to this innovation, people wrote books by hand at a rate of perhaps forty pages a day. The Gutenberg press could churn out an astonishing thirty-six hundred printed pages daily.

In 1983, computers could communicate with each other through an invention known as the internet. And not long after, in 2004, a Harvard undergraduate named Mark Zuckerberg launched Facebook, the largest social media entity in the world.

This is not about the evolution of media. Paintings, hieroglyphics, books, and the internet itself are simply tools for a higher purpose (or sometimes a lower purpose...depending on the motive of the user). The timeline above is truly about the development of storytelling.

Throughout all of human history, storytellers held positions of importance and respect. And today the storyteller class is the wealthiest and most powerful segment of our society.

Many of us equate storytelling to entertainment and, in American culture, we have several examples of success in this sector: big-time movie directors, producers, actors, writers, singers, and more. All rich and all influential beyond their individual art.

Entertainers, however, are not the only storytellers we have... or value.

Consider any large and successful company: Apple, Google, Tesla, any big company you like.

Now consider the competitors in their sector of the economy when they were starting out. This competition could come from rival companies in the same line of business, or it could be from a public that was unaware of the company's very existence and needed extensive consumer education before they would spend money on it. Whatever the case, it isn't easy to start and scale a company to the size and success of those mentioned above.

Why did they survive—and, better yet, flourish—when others (many, many others) did not? What makes them so special?

Their stories captivated people. Successful companies in every sector of the economy tell their story daily as they cultivate loyal customers. When you mention Apple, you can't help but think about Steve Jobs and his obsession with design. His story changed personal electronics forever. Google was the first search engine to capture the public's attention with its groundbreaking algorithm, all developed by two Stanford University computer science grad students. Tesla would be just another electric vehicle play if not for the attention-getting quirks of Elon Musk. Now Tesla leads the market.

They and other successful business leaders all have stories to tell. They communicate their vision for how they intend to change the world, and they do it passionately. When problems arise in the American free-enterprise economy, their stories guide them through tough times and lead them through to better days. There's no doubt Steve Jobs, Larry Page, Sergey Brin, and Elon Musk have all made mistakes that could have destroyed their companies, but they used their stories to keep moving forward, and the public rewarded them with significant wealth.

No company or organization can survive without a story. You may call it a "brand" or "identity" or "avatar" or any of the current buzzwords, but the only thing you cannot do is ignore the need.

People—individuals or in a collective, such as a community or company—have an ingrained need to connect, share, and engage with the world around them. We're not solitary creatures. The same goes for the groupings we create.

The need to communicate is primal. Success is optional. Just because you need to do something doesn't mean you'll be any good at it. Human communication is a tricky business, full of nuance and subtext.

This book is a tool for your success, which is rooted in the understanding of the **purpose, power**, and **plan** to support your public-speaking efforts.

Your purpose is all about your motivations. Why do you seek an audience? What does your message—that which you will champion and fight for—say about you as a person? Reflection is an essential part of the process.

Next, understand what makes speeches powerful. Why spend time and energy on a talk that is weak and forgettable? Wouldn't you rather understand the approach, tools, and tactics that make speeches resonate and motivate? Of course you would. Who wouldn't?

And then there's the plan. Successful speeches are not happy accidents. "Winging it" is an invitation to disaster. All professional speakers have a plan before they step up to the mic, even if they are giving what everyone believes is an "impromptu" talk.

With an understanding of purpose, power, and plan, you will craft talks and presentations that win...however you define winning. Perhaps it's earning new customers and growing your business. Maybe it's advancing a nonprofit cause you care deeply about. Or maybe it's winning over new acquaintances in social settings. Heightened speaking skills serve all of those missions and much, much more.

There's no question you can do great things as a skilled speaker. The only real question is, What can't you do with those skills?

And the answer is...nothing at all. Everything is possible.

PART 1

THE PURPOSE

"Try not to become a man of success, but rather try to become a man of value."

—ALBERT EINSTEIN, CELEBRATED GENIUS

YOU KNOW WHO YOU ARE AND WHAT YOU ARE...HOW about *why* you are? What is your purpose? It's an important enough question that we devote the first third of this book to exploring it.

"But this is a book about public speaking," you may say. "Why try to unpack one of the deeper philosophical questions a human can ask? That seems like a lot for someone who came here to learn how to give a stronger presentation at work."

If you came here for tips and tactics, no problem. You can skip ahead to the next section on the power and definitely get better on stage.

However, if you came to this book with the hope—no, the burning desire—to make a real impact with your speeches, perhaps even change the world for the better, you need to start here.

Ben Franklin, one of our more interesting Founding Fathers, once said, "There are three things extremely hard: steel, a diamond and to know oneself." Talk about being on point. We humans are a mystery to each other and ourselves. The proof of this lies in the fact that we endure a great deal of divorce, job dissatisfaction, fluctuations in diet and fitness, and other significant life management challenges. Would we have all that if we truly understood ourselves?

We struggle to find and identify the meaning and purpose in our lives. It's not that we don't care. We care very deeply.

No, the problem is that finding purpose is a tough job. Our messy, complicated lives, jobs, and relationships shroud the process in thick smoke, making the way forward difficult to see.

Still, it's vital. Your speeches will matter only if you are truly standing for what you believe, what you passionately care about and understand even better than anyone else around. Purpose is one of the few forces on the planet strong enough to fuel a campaign like that.

So let's spend some time seeing if we can find your purpose and/or further refine the one you have.

CHAPTER 1

WHY DO SPEAKERS NEED PURPOSE?

IN A STATEMENT THAT IS BOTH OBVIOUS AND PROFOUND, American author Robert Byrne once wrote, "The purpose of life is a life of purpose."[1] Purpose is one of those things we vaguely know is good. We're not aware of anyone who is antipurpose.

However, if you don't know the specific, observable, measurable benefits and the meaning, you may not find the right motivation to do the work of uncovering your still-undefined purpose. You will find more research than you can process on this very topic with only a cursory web search.

To save time, we'll lay out just a sampling of what we found.

A 2021 article in *Psychology Today* ("Is Purpose or Pleasure the Key to Happiness as We Age?") gives synopses of several studies. In summary, the article states, "People with purpose tend to be happier, healthier, and even wealthier. They are more likely to practice

---

[1] Robert Byrne, "21," in *The Third—and Possibly the Best—637 Best Things Anybody Ever Said*, ed. Robert Byrne (New York: Atheneum, 1986), 4.

healthy habits, sleep better, enjoy stronger personal relationships, and have better mental health. Moreover, they have a reduced risk of Alzheimer's."[2]

The article says the happiness one receives from their sense of purpose is enduring happiness, lasting longer than the happiness that comes from pleasurable activities.

A study published in the *Journal of the American Medical Association* undertook a meta-analysis of data compiled by the University of Michigan Health and Retirement Study, which has been following the health metrics of approximately twenty thousand US adults over the age of fifty since 1992. The study analyzed HRS data regarding the psychological well-being of 6,985 participants gathered between 2006 and 2010. The results showed a strong association between purpose in life and decreased mortality among older Americans.[3]

A follow-up study by the same university in 2010 clearly demonstrated that working with a sense of purpose leads to significantly greater engagement, motivation, productivity, and retention on the job.

A psychology professor at Carleton University in Ottawa, Canada, named Patrick Hill followed six thousand people in the United States over the course of fourteen years. He wanted to see the effect of purpose on lifespan. Hill found that "for every one standard deviation increase in purpose, the risk of dying over the next fourteen years diminished by 15 percent."[4] This was after accounting

---

[2] Meg Selig, "Is Purpose or Pleasure the Key to Happiness as We Age?: For Happiness at Any Age, Try These 7 Ways to Blend Purpose and Pleasure," Psychology Today, November 1, 2021, https://www.psychologytoday.com/us/blog/changepower/202111/is-purpose-or-pleasure-the-key-happiness-we-age.

[3] Aliya Alimujiang et al., "Association between Life Purpose and Mortality among US Adults Older than 50 Years," *JAMA Network Open* 2, no. 5 (May 2019): e194270, https://doi.org/10.1001/jamanetworkopen.2019.4270.

[4] Patrick L. Hill and Nicholas A. Turiano, "Purpose in Life as a Predictor of Mortality across Adulthood," *Psychological Science* 25, no. 7 (2014): 1485, https://doi.org/10.1177/0956797614531799.

for other factors that affected life longevity. The study also found purpose had a benefit for the individual regardless of when they adopted it. Purpose seemed to extend the life of those who found it in their twenties, thirties, middle age, and beyond.[5]

Hill seems to believe that purpose may protect a person from the harmful effects of stress, which is known to cause early aging and premature death.

Anthony Burrow, a psychologist at Cornell University, tested that assumption.[6] He conducted an experiment where some students journaled their feelings while experiencing known stressors and others watched movies. The results tracked what one would expect, except for students who wrote about having a sense of purpose in their journal entries. They reported no feelings of increased stress despite being exposed to known stressors. Burrow's takeaway: a sense of purpose seems to protect against the negative effects of stress.[7]

To recap, purpose is scientifically linked to longer, happier, and more satisfying lives.

Does this interest you?

Purpose is not a pill one takes to passively get an effect. Purpose is work. Living with purpose means living for purpose, always supporting your specific reason for being with your labors, your studies, and your words.

We speak because we feel drawn by a primal need to advance that which serves our life's purpose. That purpose is different from the purposes of your family members, friends, and coworkers. Yet those

---

5   Hill and Turiano, "Purpose in Life," 1482–1486.

6   Bronfenbrenner Center for Translational Research, "'Knowing Your Why' Is Good for You," *Evidence-Based Living* (blog), Cornell University, accessed July 23, 2024, https://evidencebasedliving.human.cornell.edu/blog/knowing-your-why-is-good-for-you/.

7   Jackie Swift, "The Benefits of Having a Sense of Purpose," Medium, December 7, 2020, https://cornellresearch.medium.com/the-benefits-of-having-a-sense-of-purpose-ae05232cf5c8.

who have embraced their purpose—the quintessential "why" of their lives—all feel the same pull. Your outlet can be public speaking, taking the passion and purpose that improves your life and sharing it with others. Put another way, speeches are opportunities for you to show others what is real for you. You make it a gift to them in the hopes it will add value to their lives.

Some individuals pursue public speaking opportunities for less honorable motives. Some speakers, particularly successful ones, exploit the microphone to profit from unsuspecting individuals. Others may use their platform to champion falsehoods in pursuing a misguided agenda. Political hacks, unproven medical cure hucksters, science and history deniers—they are all out there, getting the unfortunate attention of audiences.

They make the world a darker, less trusting place.

Then there are the exceptional entertainers who possess the ability to momentarily uplift your spirits but ultimately leave you unable to recall their words. They are not evil, simply producers of "cotton candy" communication: quickly consumed and then forgotten.

A person's genuine purpose—irrespective of fame or financial gain—is the truest reason for public speaking. It is crucial that the person with the biggest and most credible vision has the most influence in a room with others.

CHAPTER 2

WHY DO SPEAKERS NEED VALUES?

SCOTT MANN IS A RETIRED LIEUTENANT COLONEL WITH the Green Beret Special Forces unit of the Army. He is also a respected authority on leadership whom we have had the pleasure of training with over the years.

Scott recognizes that even in today's modern world, with all our technology and sophistication, people still identify themselves through tribes. Tribalism is a different take on community, as there are stronger ties with tribes versus other types of communities. This creates a deeper feeling of devotion and personal investment.

Tribes align not based on geography, or politics, or even religion. Rather, they form along the ties of shared values. Overlap frequently occurs as members of a religion or faith community commonly share values. Often, we view our values through filters and then cluster them for the organization's sake. We identify religious values, business values, family values, patriotic values, etc. Yet the values themselves act as the unifying force that creates these resilient tribes.

Once you have discovered your tribe and sense your deep

connection to it, there are no boundaries to the extent of your dedication to the tribe. You will sacrifice your comfort and possessions if necessary. You would even die for your tribe. Such is its strength.

Love, compassion, persistence, devotion, and wisdom make up a small sampling of values one may hold precious. There are numerous additional ones. According to Scott, you will seek kindred spirits based on whatever values rise highest in your preferences and priorities.

What does this have to do with giving a speech?

In an interesting article for *Inc.* magazine, writer Adam Fridman says, "Purpose inspires. Values guide. Habits define. Purpose is about why we do what we do, [v]alues are how we achieve purpose. Habits are what we do every day that reflects our purpose and values. Habits are purpose and values made visible."[8]

Values guide. They will guide you as you create speeches that serve your purpose in life.

---

8   Adam Fridman, "Four Essential Habits to Align Purpose and Values with Actions," *Inc.*, June 15, 2017, https://www.inc.com/adam-fridman/four-essential-habits-to-align-purpose-and-values-with-actions.html.

CHAPTER 3

USING ASSESSMENTS TO CLARIFY ONE'S PURPOSE AND VALUES

FRANKLIN HAS ALREADY STATED IT, AND WE WILL REITerate: knowing oneself is exceedingly difficult. In our perspective, you have three paths to choose from as you seek self-knowledge. Trust us; they are worth it.

The reason we are so focused on psychology in a public speaking book is that once you figure yourself out—truly understand your purpose, your values, and your ultimate goals as a person and as a speaker—you will become authentic.

Consider this: when speaking before a group of strangers, you start with nothing. We know that people must establish a rapport before they take one another seriously and, more importantly, trust one another.

That is a tough place to get to under normal circumstances, when you have time to develop a relationship with others.

However, the speaker has some time constraints. You can't take the day getting to know your audience. You must establish rapport within a matter of minutes (seconds) or you are going to lose their attention.

Authenticity allows you to connect with people very quickly. Once you connect, people will trust and believe you. And once you have passed through that gate, you are able to motivate others to action or to think differently about something you care about... your choice.

Another benefit of understanding yourself better is enhanced decision-making. When you know what you are about—and, equally important, what you are against—your life becomes simpler. Not easy, no one has an easy life (which would be pretty boring, truth be told), but definitely simpler. Because when you truly know yourself, life's decisions are almost premade. You'll spend less time agonizing in indecision and more time doing.

All of which brings us back to the three paths for achieving this understanding of self.

First, you can go it alone. It may be a bit like reinventing the wheel, considering the abundance of thinkers who have thoroughly documented the promising trials and the dead ends in these areas. Perhaps you are one of those original thinkers who want to reflect in isolation and find your own way. If so, we'd love to hear what you discover someday.

Second, you can enlist the help of mentors and coaches. We are big believers in the power of mentorship. Greg, especially, has developed a network of professionals he can go to for help to get to the next level of skill development. After more than thirty years of communications work, we are acutely aware there is always a higher level.

One coach stands out. Jonathan Altfeld, a GeniusMapping™ expert and coach, is truly exceptional. He has a gift for helping anyone find and understand their values and life goals. (We encourage you to check out his website: geniusmapping.com.) Working with a mentor or coach cuts down on the time and stress associated with self-discovery. You get further down the path faster.

Honestly, there are expenses to consider. Professionals deserve compensation for what they bring to their clients. Maybe you are lucky enough to have a personal or social relationship with a potential mentor. Free mentors are fantastic. If you know someone with significant experience and skills who will help you at no cost, say "Thank you" and listen. However, assuming your social network doesn't include the caliber of professional you need for growth, you must be prepared to pay...and it won't be cheap...nor should it be.

The third path can give you results without the ongoing expense. This route uses assessments. A legitimate, well-executed assessment will provide incredible insights into your inner strengths, passions, talents, and aptitudes.

A STORY FROM GREG

Years ago, I wanted to pursue public speaking...and I was not very good at it at all. My first few attempts were failures, and I resigned myself to the conventional wisdom that if I tried it a few times and couldn't find success, it just wasn't meant for me.

Except I couldn't stop thinking about it. My mind kept pulling me in that ruinous direction. I felt completely frustrated with having a deep passion for something I appeared to be completely unsuccessful at.

Then I discovered the PRO-D assessment from TAI Incorporated. I already had experience in assessments through my personal study of leadership and management. Over the years, I have explored and tried several personality and strength/talent assessments. All provided some value. It was when I discovered PRO-D that I could resolve the frustration over public speaking that I had suffered with for too long.

That assessment correctly identified the fact that I really did have some underlying talent in public speaking. I simply didn't have enough training to use it effectively.

That revelation made all the difference in my life and set me on the path I am enjoying today.

Recommended Assessments:

- PRO-D by TAI incorporated—Pro-d.com
- *StrengthsFinder 2.0* by Tom Rath and Gallup—gallup.com
- *StandOut 2.0* by Marcus Buckingham—book available on Amazon
- The WHY Institute—whyinstitute.com

Assessments will surprise you. They will give you insights into your personal values and overall purpose in life. However, should you decide to take the first path and discover yourself on your own, we'd like to suggest some helpful questions you can use in the process:

1. What do you stand for? (Integrity, forgiveness, authenticity, love, growth, learning, connection, faith, health...)
2. What do you oppose? (Greed, self-centeredness, apathy, mediocrity, dishonesty, manipulation, instant gratification, victimhood...)
3. Of all the positive impacts you have had on others throughout your life, which is the one that makes you most proud?

4. Of all the hindrances you have had to face, which is the biggest hindrance you must fight against repeatedly to keep making your most positive impact?
5. What are your strengths, skills, and knowledge beyond your natural talents?
6. What do you most enjoy learning about?
7. What are the things you are completely passionate about right now?
8. When you pursue your passion, what happens? What doesn't happen?
9. When you don't pursue your passion, what happens? What doesn't happen?
10. During what activity do you feel the greatest sense of "self"?
11. Describe your friends. What characteristics do you most admire in them? Do you share those characteristics?
12. What makes you laugh? Do you have sources of joy in your life? What joy do you bring to others?
13. What makes you cry? Do you have the capacity for compassion? Do you act on it?
14. If you were to write a mission statement or eulogy about your life, what would it say? How do you think people who know you would respond to it?
15. What makes you sing?
16. What makes you dance with abandon and without embarrassment?
17. What are your favorite movies, documentaries, or books? Of the top five, what themes are common among them?

The honest answers to these questions will paint a clear and vivid picture of the person you really are. We hope you like and appreciate what you find.

If you want additional guidance on self-discovery, we suggest you read *The Purpose Factor* by Brian and Gabrielle Boshé (a book we like so much, we'll reference it again in a few pages).

CHAPTER 4

THE MESSAGE

PUBLIC SPEAKING IS A LINEAR PROCESS. FIRST YOU IDENtify your purpose and work to understand it. Then you take stock of your values, making sure you understand them clearly and appreciate how they can (and will) guide your speeches.

Then—and only then—do you craft your message.

Now you get to work distilling the essence of "you" into a message that others can benefit from. This is the first iteration of what will become your speech. We have some content creation help for you coming up.

For now, think about your messaging as a way to share what's important inside you with others in a way that is both easily understood and completely irresistible.

You begin by creating a message that you would want to hear. One that is authentic for you. Anything else is a waste of time.

Then you must find the language that fulfills both your message and your audience's needs. It's important to remember you will have expertise in your subject that the audience doesn't. It can be tempting for professionals to slip into jargon specific to their expertise. Jargon is the shorthand professionals use when speaking with peers, not outsiders. Figure out a way to translate what you know so those outside your circle will understand it.

Language, as well as everything else in that speech, serves the message. This is not about vanity but keeping a focus on creating something of value for the audience. This matters more than the ancillary benefits you may get from giving the speech, such as money and notoriety. If you land on a message that genuinely serves your purpose as guided by your values, it will make a significant impact.

TEACHINGS ABOUT MESSAGE FROM MAXWELL

"When you find your mission, you find your voice."

—JOHN MAXWELL

Here's where we transition from purpose—the essence of who you are—to mission—your action state. It's what you do in service of your purpose. It's important to know that mission and purpose are different things, both of which need to be respected and utilized if you are to become the speaker you aspire to be.

The mission is articulated and advanced through messaging.

John Maxwell, the world-renowned leadership expert and speaker—and mentor to Greg—talks about messages nested within messages in his book *The 16 Undeniable Laws of Communication*. These are called the "big message." This one never changes. It is consistent because it focuses on your audience. They, in their collective, are the ones you serve. They're the boss. Therefore, it is crucial that you prioritize considering four significant questions when serving them.

1. What do you want them to see?
2. What do you want them to think?
3. What do you want them to feel?
4. What do you want them to do?

The answers to those questions must align with your mission and, more specifically, your values as a human being. Your origin story also shaped this "big message," that unique-in-the-world journey that made you the person (speaker) you are.

So, before we get into the best messages you embed into the big message, let's take a brief detour into another set of authors we admire and learn from.

Brian and Gabrielle Bosché's book *The Purpose Factor* provides a wealth of insights into what makes a person. Not the physical but the intangibles. Here's an overview of how they break it down.

First, you have your "natural advantage," your "acquired skills," your "pull passion," and your unique "origin story."

Your natural advantage determines how you are wired. Some examples include people who are natural builders, who can create with their hands; truthtellers, those unafraid to speak the truth; recruiters, those folks who enjoy rallying people for an effort; overseers, who enjoy managing that work; and teachers, those driven by a desire to help others grow and learn. We could name others, but you get the idea. Whatever we gravitate to, we find what we can do with minimal stress and maximum success. This encompasses our natural advantage.

Acquired skills are supporting skills. They are things we learned along the way to facilitate the use of our natural advantage skills. They are how we use what comes naturally.

Brian and Gabrielle's ideas on passion are interesting. We all can appreciate how powerful a force passion is. It's a huge driver in all our lives. Brian and Gabrielle refined the notion of passion more specifically into two different types: push and pull.

Passions that you must push through—those requiring a lot of effort to realize—are fleeting. While many of us admire the results of hard work, no one wants to work harder than they must. Such is the case with push passions. They burn bright and fast.

Pull passions are different. These are the great loves that pull us through life. These passions endure because we don't have to sweat—or even take much notice—in order to make them happen.

An origin story is as it sounds: the amalgamation of all that has happened in your life to make you "you" and create the life force that drives you daily.

Got it? Alright, let's get back to Maxwell.

You already know you have your big message, that tried-and-true overarching concern that never changes. Into this shell, Maxwell talks about inserting your best messages...those daily concerns, whatever is on your mind that you feel the need to speak on. These do change, sometimes a lot. If you take on speaking engagements over a long enough stretch of time, you may very well generate thousands of these messages.

There's nothing wrong with that. It's great...so long as you don't forget the big message. That has to be there. That concern for the needs of your audience, tempered by your origin story and values, is the golden thread that must run through everything because without it, you don't have authenticity. And if you are not relatable and believable, what good is it being up on that stage? After decades of reflecting, writing, and coaching leaders all around the world, Maxwell knows the answer: there is no benefit—no point—to public speaking without authority, authenticity, and transparency.

Maxwell also shares an excellent approach in using these observations. It's this: don't unload your important messages on the audience without "ramp time." What he means is that you need to take the time to form connections with your listeners first, before you can ask them to accept your big and best messages. You may need to warm them up, if you will. Like starting your car in the dead of winter. You can't just jump on the gas and screech out of the parking lot the second you turn on the ignition. You may need to wait a bit. Let it warm up. Then you're ready to cruise.

SERVANT SPEAKER

John Maxwell knows the best leaders in the world are servant leaders. We're talking about those who put their people before themselves. It's those special bosses who know how to care for those who follow them and, as a result, earn tremendous loyalty.

Just like servant leaders, there are also servant speakers who serve.

According to Maxwell, when you start off as a speaker, you naturally make the exercise 75 percent about you, 20 percent about the content, and 5 percent about the audience. All of that is understandable. It takes a fair bit of ego to put yourself out in front of others.

However, once you become experienced and realize the purpose of speaking is to help other people, those percentages flip. Seasoned speakers make it 75 percent about the audience, 20 percent content, and the remaining 5 percent is about themselves.

Perhaps the best way to think about this is by imagining your talk (and by "talk" we are including everything from your time to prepare for the insights you eventually share) as a gift. Your abilities, intelligence, and energy are gifts you have a responsibility to share. Some audiences may warmly receive your gift, others may not know quite how to accept it, but either way, you need to stay humble and in a mind frame of service because *you* are not the gift. Your skill, information, attitude, and more make up the gift you give, but you are simply the vessel. It's important to separate the two; otherwise, you risk making your speeches about you and what you need. Selfish speakers offer no value to others.

CHAPTER 5

MIND YOUR MINDSET

SPEAKERS LIVE IN SIMILAR WORLDS THAN THOSE OF writers and other creatives. Eventually, they fling open the doors guarding their worlds and share the creation they have worked so long and hard on in a public way.

Prior to that moment, the speaker's world is solitary. It's you and your thoughts. Thoughts can easily and rapidly transform into words and messages. Relish those times as they are precious and few.

Most of the time you will spend alone, wrestling with a jumble of ideas in your mind, trying to make sense of it all. That struggle is worthy of your time. Great material comes from it. As you work on your core messages, there are some matters of mindset that can help. We offer you these thoughts in hopes that they help you manage yours.

WHAT IF

If you were to pick your life's top three priorities, what would they be? And do your actions—how you live your life every day—align with those priorities? Those are big questions that are difficult to answer without some thought.

Let's try this: imagine you had all the money and time you could possibly use. In fact, let's go a step further and think about how it would be if we knew we could not fail. Feels nice, doesn't it? Now, with that as your background, what would you spend your time on?

The things we spend our time, treasure, and talent on voluntarily are the most valuable pursuits in our lives...even without unlimited time and funds.

Go a step further in this exercise and check out your bank statement. Look and see where you spent your money. There will be a list of life realities you can't escape—mortgages, groceries, and the like. That's the routine, daily living stuff we do to survive.

Look instead at what you are choosing to do with your resources. Look at what you spend money on by choice. Check your planner or calendar to see what you willingly invest your time in. We treat time cheaply...way too cheaply. It's the one resource we can't create more of. Your personal time, separate from work or other obligations, holds immense value. Hopefully, you're spending that precious time on worthy things.

Are you, in fact, spending your time and financial resources (whatever they may be) on efforts that line up with your life's purpose, mission, and values?

If it matters to you in life, you should reflect it in the speeches you make. These choices, perhaps, reflect your values, providing more clues to the mystery of what drives you. What are your purchases and appointments saying about your values?

HAPPINESS AND JOY

Depressed people cannot imagine positive stories for their future. As such, they are not in the best mind frame for public speaking. (Of course, there are exceptions. Someone speaking from personal experience about the importance of mental health, for example.)

You don't need a study to prove the world is in short supply of joy. There is no group advocating otherwise.

And what is joy?

In today's consumer culture, it's easy to confuse short-term happiness with joy, but there is a difference.

Happiness can be a fleeting feeling, something momentarily achieved in a variety of ways. Watching a comedy special on TV can make you feel happy at the moment. Then, once the program is over and real life returns, the laughter stops and the smile fades.

Genuine joy is an enduring feeling of safety and peace. It is a state of existence that empowers you to freely express yourself without boundaries and enables you to both give and receive love without conditions.

We don't need to tell you which one is the preferred state.

It stands to reason that if your audiences have less joy in their lives, as most people do, they will crave more. And if your speech helps them realize even a small fraction of more true joy in their lives after hearing it, they will remember, respect, and love you for a very long time.

Speeches are about serving the audience information and feeling. Give them what they want and need if you're able.

And any pro speaker will tell you, this is also a source of real joy—to know a group of people who are honestly happy to see you and eager to hear your wisdom and perspective. This is joyful for any speaker. Keep this in mind as you prepare and craft future speeches: work brings joy.

KNOW YOUR ROLE AND RELATIONSHIP WITH THE AUDIENCE

"The most important function of the speaker is giving the audience what they need at that time."

—MARY KINCAID, WRITER, SPEAKER, AND STORYTELLER

People like organization. They need it. When we don't know our role or purpose, we get confused, and before long, we have problems. Mild confusion is wonderful because it elicits curiosity...maybe even anticipation. Actual confusion serves only to frustrate, worry, and scare people.

Big organizations—from corporations to our armed forces—simply could not function without all participants having a clear understanding of their role.

The same clarity of purpose also enables successful speeches. The proper role of the speaker is to be a servant. As Mary Kincaid notes above, you must give your audience what they need at that time.[9]

It may seem like we are encouraging you to compromise your values. There is, however, a difference between giving people what they need and pandering. Pandering is changing who you are in order to be liked. It's the misguided work of giving people what you think they want without regard for anything beyond your benefit. And there's the difference. Sometimes people need and want the same thing at the same time, but when they don't, you're free to ignore the want.

What you give people as a speaker doesn't ever really change, because that "thing"—whatever it may be—is what you authentically have to give. The only thing that really changes is your delivery based on the details of your audience.

What gives you that authority? You do. You're the speaker, and

---

[9] Mary Kincaid, direct communication with the author.

you're obligated to give speeches you would want to hear based on your experiences and values. That internal measure is your quality control. It's also a matter of authenticity. If you do not give your listeners the benefit of your true self, you're giving them something less than genuine, and they deserve better.

Your expertise and perspectives are gifts to be given. If they are honest, they are exactly what people need.

Now that you know your role, what are you? Let's spend a moment on what you are not.

You are not your speech. That may be strange to hear and internalize. After all, you care about what you came to talk about, and if you're doing it right, you invested a lot of time and energy into that talk. It would be quite natural to identify with your speech, maybe even consider it a part of you, an actual extension of your being.

Professionals understand there must be a division. You are not your speech. You are the creator and the voice, but the speech is its own entity.

There is a "love triangle," if you will, consisting of you, your content, and your audience. They are three separate things connected at a moment in time.

You have a relationship with your content, and you have a distinct relationship with your audience. The same thing goes for your audience and your content. The three of you stand self-reliant and interconnected.

That becomes important because the separate relationships between you all bring different benefits. Your relationship with the audience ensures you serve them well, as Mary Kincaid suggests. Your relationship with the content confirms your expertise, while ensuring you don't "sell out" and alter the content to pander to anyone.

Know this: everyone hears a different speech. If you were to deliver a talk and subsequently interview and survey each member of the audience, you would discover a multitude of interpretations for your speech, equal to the number of listeners.

We would also like to point out that pausing is a vital part of this process. When your intent is to be a true servant speaker and give your audience value in your message/story, it is important for you to pause from time to time so the audience can absorb your words and reflect on their meaning. You are, after all, introducing them to new thoughts, and that takes time to process. If you are mindful to give your audience enough breaks for this processing to occur, they become de facto "co-creators" of your talk. They'll understand more of what you are saying and start filling in any gaps in the message you may have inadvertently left behind. By actively participating in the process, they become invested and derive far more value from the time spent together than if they had been rushed through.

FUTURE SELF

The idea of doing things now that your future self will thank you for has been used quite a bit by the diet and fitness industries. It also applies well to public speaking.

What world are you trying to create for your future self? What goals can your future self accomplish through public speaking?

This is one of the wonderful aspects of becoming a regular speaker: you don't have a boss you're answerable to. You only need to seek the approval of your future self. Keep this in mind as you look for speaking opportunities and when creating those talks. Are you doing what your future self would approve of? Make sure you check in with him or her (your future self) from time to time and make sure you are on the right track.

Try this as an exercise. Sit in a quiet place. Close your eyes. Now picture yourself twenty years from now doing what you aspire to be doing with your life. Don't cheat yourself—dream big. Now think about what advice your older self would give your current self to get to that desired place in your life. Then listen to yourself! Follow that advice to the letter.

Part 2

THE POWER

"Speech isn't just about communicating ideas or opinions. Sometimes, it is about trying to convey whole human lives."

—DENNIS LEHANE, *MYSTIC RIVER*

IT WAS EARLY 1775, AND THE AMERICAN COLONISTS WERE furious. A barrage of new taxes levied by Britain's Townshend and Stamp Acts seemed grossly unfair, and a war was brewing. Massachusetts was ready to fight. Virginia was not.

British armed forces were the most powerful in the world, and though passions ran high, many early Americans were terrified of taking on an invincible enemy. The colonists would need to be united if they were to stand any chance against Britain, but Virginia remained on the fence.

Patrick Henry, an attorney, farmer, and statesman in early Virginia, wasn't having it. Speaking before the state convention, Henry gave his famous "Give me liberty or give me death" speech...the one we all learned about in elementary school history. That speech not only convinced Virginia to join the war effort, but it also gave additional motivation and strength to both George Washington and Thomas Jefferson, who were in attendance and would go on to play major roles in the founding of our country.

ANOTHER SPEECH THAT CHANGED AMERICA: THE CIVIL WAR

November 19, 1863. The American Civil War had been raging for two years and, just a few months earlier, had marked its bloodiest battle yet in Gettysburg, Pennsylvania. President Abraham Lincoln came to Gettysburg to commemorate that awful battle and honor the dead. He delivered a 272-word speech, beginning with "Fourscore and seven years ago our fathers brought forth, on this continent, a new nation, conceived in liberty, and dedicated to the proposition that all men are created equal." It would change the course of the war and keep the country united.

(Interesting side note for you. Many believe Lincoln wrote this speech on the train to Gettysburg, giving the impression that the president "threw it together" quickly. However, famed presidential historian Doris Kearns Goodwin, in her book *Team of Rivals*, says Lincoln worked on the Gettysburg Address for months. He sweated the details because anyone can ramble, but a true wordsmith knows it takes more work—not less—to write a concise, powerful talk.)

AND ANOTHER...

In 1963 during the March on Washington, as the country was grappling with the issues of racial fairness and justice—and trying to quell the violence that followed the discussion all over America—an

Atlanta preacher named Martin Luther King Jr. peacefully gave his famous "I Have a Dream" speech before 250,000 people. Soon after that, Congress passed both the Civil Rights Act and the Voting Rights Act.

"The only thing we have to fear...is fear itself." "Mr. Gorbachev, tear down this wall." "Ask not what your country can do for you... ask what you can do for your country."

American history is replete with speeches that literally changed both the country and the world. And these are just a few of the domestic examples. There are speeches made by men and women throughout history who have created the world we inhabit today. These speakers were not all elected leaders, nor were they all classically educated, wealthy, or necessarily the beneficiaries of any other advantages. The only truly common thread that connects them all is passion for their vision of a better world and an understanding of—and commitment to—the very power of speeches.

Great speeches don't just create change; they demand it. The power of the words and the ideas they define is formidable. They demand attention and leave a lasting impact.

You may someday give a speech to rival the Gettysburg Address. It could happen.

Or maybe you won't. That's fine too. Because when you understand the power behind successful speeches and you learn how to use it, you will create a change in your corner of the world: your social circle, organization, community, etc. We don't have to be Henry, Lincoln, or King to be powerful agents of change. Your ideas, words, and commitment are more than enough.

CHAPTER 6

STORY

RELIGION, BOOKS, SONGS, MOVIES, FAMILY GENEALOGIES, political campaigns, and corporate advertising. These distinct things all share one significant commonality: they all require story to spread out and take root in the hearts and minds of people.

Story is the most powerful medium in human communication. Period. Understanding this will make you an extraordinary speaker. From the time when our distant ancestors gathered around campfires and shared tales to the modern day, the story has been what we love and what we need. And after millennia of relying on story to help us understand ourselves and the world, our brains have become hardwired to seek stories.

Stories change lives. They can also be big business. In 1986, Apple founder Steve Jobs bought a computer graphics company with partners and renamed the enterprise Pixar. Jobs understood early the appeal of good storytelling through animation, and Pixar churned out big commercial hits like *Toy Story*. When Jobs sold Pixar to the Walt Disney Company in 2006, the purchase price was 14,000 percent greater than the initial investment. Such is the power (and worth) of story. Disney had the option to acquire other graphics companies, but finding storytellers as exceptional as Pixar is exceedingly rare and valuable.

We believe stories shape and change lives in profound ways.

Here's what writer and storyteller Christine Hennebury had to say about story in a piece she wrote for the Canadian Broadcasting Corporation:[10]

> Storytelling is a fundamental part of being human. Stories let us share information in a way that creates an emotional connection.
>
> They help us to understand that information and each other, and it makes the information memorable.
>
> Because stories create an emotional connection, we can gain a deeper understanding of other people's experiences.
>
> That not only helps us to understand their lives but allows us to take the lessons they have learned and apply it to our own.

Author Tom Corson-Knowles calls stories "central to human cognition and communication" and says we are all automatically drawn to stories because we see ourselves reflected in them.[11] Corson-Knowles cites six reasons why stories matter even today, in the age of reason and computers.

---

10 Christine Hennebury, "Storytelling Is Not Just Entertainment. It's a Fundamental Part of Being Human," CBC News, March 29, 2020, https://www.cbc.ca/news/canada/newfoundland-labrador/storytelling-is-human-1.5511027.

11 Tom Corson-Knowles, "Stories Matter: Why Stories Are Important to Our Lives and Culture," TCK Publishing, accessed July 23, 2024, https://www.tckpublishing.com/stories-matter/.

1. Stories are universal. They span cultures and help us find commonality with others.
2. Stories help us understand our unique place in the world.
3. Stories help us learn how to act wisely.
4. Stories help shape our perspective of the world.
5. Stories help us understand other people and their perspectives.
6. Stories pass down knowledge and morals.

A STORY FROM GREG

My father was a deeply patriotic man who loved his country. One of the many ways he displayed his devotion was flying the American flag on a pole at our home. Dad flew his flag proudly all day long. Back then, in 1980s Ohio, respectful citizens did not fly their flags at night without lighting. We did not have lighting for our flag, so my father would faithfully and lovingly lower the flag each day at dusk and store it until after dawn the following day.

One day, I got the idea that I would help my father and take the flag down for him. I was around fifteen at the time—young enough that my priority was saving my father some time with the chore rather than doing the chore correctly.

I ran out to the pole, lowered the flag, grabbed it, and ran inside, where I thought my dad would be grateful for the assist.

Dad met me at the door and was as angry as I had ever seen him. You should know, I've only seen my father truly angry three times in my entire life. This was one of them. He was as angry as a hornet.

Instead, he ordered me upstairs to my room. He was not appreciative. He was mad, and I couldn't understand why.

The next morning, Dad came to my room and said, "Get dressed. You're not going to school today. You're coming with me." There was no further explanation. And during the five-hour car ride that followed, he didn't speak to me. A few times I tried to break the mood by asking, "Where are we going?" And my dad would only respond with "You'll see." That was the longest trip of my life, although I have driven far more miles on trips before and after this one. That ride in my father's silence was insufferably long.

Eventually we rounded a corner, and I saw the Washington Monument and I knew our destination.

We stopped when we got to Arlington National Cemetery, and my father told me to get out of the car. We were on a little rise of a hill, and I could see the white grave markers in their neat rows, stretching far into the distance.

My father turned to me and said, "Stay here until you can tell me why all these soldiers died." This total experience seemed to have come out of nowhere, and I was shocked by it all, but I wanted to make my father happy again, so I stood there awhile and tried to think.

I eventually came back to him, in the car, and said, "They died for our freedom, right?" Dad looked at me and said, "No, Greg. There are soldiers all over the world who fight for their notion of freedom. These soldiers died for your dreams. They protect your dreams to be anything you want, and this is the only country on earth where it happens. That's why I was upset with you last night. You didn't take care of the flag that they served and died for. Instead, you dragged it on the ground."

Today, our company gives generously to veterans' causes. We take time to celebrate those who served before coming to work for us. And I have treated the American flag with the utmost respect every day since that day.

This need for story is true in both our personal and professional lives.

Writers Vanessa Boris and Lani Peterson, PsyD, psychologists and professional storytellers, co-wrote the following in a 2017 article for *Harvard Business Publishing* titled "What Makes Storytelling So Effective for Learning?"[12]

> Telling stories is one of the most powerful means that leaders have to influence, teach, and inspire. What makes storytelling so effective for learning? For starters, storytelling forges connections among people, and between people and ideas. Stories convey the culture, history, and values that unite people. When it comes to our countries, our communities, and our families, we understand intuitively that the stories we hold in common are an important part of the ties that bind.
>
> This understanding also holds true in the business world, where an organization's stories, and the stories its leaders tell, help solidify relationships in a way that factual statements encapsulated in bullet points or numbers don't.

---

12 Vanessa Boris and Lani Peterson, "What Makes Storytelling So Effective for Learning?," *Harvard Business Publishing: Corporate Learning* (blog), Harvard Business School, December 20, 2017, https://www.harvardbusiness.org/what-makes-storytelling-so-effective-for-learning/.

No one is eager to read a stat sheet (anxious, maybe, because there's money on the line, but never eager), yet we all love stories. What else can educate and entertain us so powerfully and in equal measure?

CHAPTER 7

PERSONAL STORY

PLENTY OF FOLKS HAVE MADE VERY NICE LIVINGS BY telling other people's stories; think writers, movie producers, and actors. There's absolutely nothing wrong with sharing a story that is not yours. That experience has value.

You, as a speaker, can share another's story—either in part or in total.

Except we're guessing that's not why you picked up this book.

Now, especially after the earlier chapter on self-discovery, you come to public speaking as a way of telling *your* story. You want to give a speech about your experiences, perspectives, and knowledge.

Let's add something to that list: your struggles.

Because a personal story is the most potent form of a communication for the speaker, and these stories cannot simply glorify you, they must be honest and authentic.

Vulnerability is a feeling most of us avoid at all costs. That idea of being exposed to ridicule or, even worse, physical harm repels and frightens us. Well, we're here to tell you that your vulnerabilities are your biggest source of strength.

Sharing the imperfect about you builds empathy in your audience. We see ourselves in stories and we all recognize that we are flawed beings. Being in the presence of another confessed imperfect person creates a kinship. We are the same.

Also, vulnerability and the candor necessary to share it builds trust. If you think about it, in our country—right now—we are severely trust depleted. Our politics have made us all wary of each other. We suspect someone's motive and grow more and more distrusting of our fellow citizens. (This, we're afraid, is true of everyone, regardless of political affiliation. You'd think we could come together and bond over that, at least. But no.)

Trust is an essential building prerequisite for public speaking. If your audience doesn't trust you and deem you honest, it will disregard what you have to say, and your cause will suffer for it. Open yourself, knowing that we all have failed and we are all less than we aspire to be. If you base your speech on your personal story, people will receive it well.

The side benefit here is that no one else can give that speech. Your personal story originates from your very specific background—from your upbringing to the present day. Of the billions of people on the planet, only you have lived through your exact set of circumstances and experiences. You have a unique personal story; it cannot be replicated. There may be others similar to it, but not precisely like it.

A STORY FROM GREG

I grew up near Youngstown, Ohio, near Canton, home of the Pro Football Hall of Fame. Football was—and still is—a big deal there, and I grew up playing regular pickup games of football with my friends. This was a regular after-school activity.

One day during our regular game, this kid Billy hit me with a vicious tackle (by the way, we played without helmets and pads). He "rang my bell" as the old-timers say, and it took me a minute to get up. I was hurting.

Billy was pretty happy with himself, and I could tell by the satisfied look on his face (he seemed to enjoy that I was in pain) that this wouldn't be the last time he would deck me. It wasn't. The abuse lasted all afternoon long. (Back then, we didn't rat out kids who were mean to us. We were the sons of steelworkers who expected us to become "Youngstown tough.")

Unfortunately, my tangles with Billy didn't end that day, nor were they confined to the football field. Now he targeted me at school. He would bully me by pushing me down stairs, tripping me, and shoving me into lockers.

I did my best to avoid him. After all, there is a difference between being tough and being stupid. I'd avoid confrontation if I could. I even walked a full mile out of my way going home one afternoon just to avoid Billy. It didn't work. He ended up ambushing me from behind a tree and hit me in the eye with a stick.

The end of it came one day when class let out and Billy came up from behind me and put me in a headlock. Enough was enough. I made a fist and swung it as hard as I could over my shoulder, and Billy went down with a thud. I knocked him out.

When he came to, he saw me and asked, "What are you still doing here?" I told him I stuck around to make sure he was OK, and after that we were friends again.

Back to normal games of friendly football.

Three years later, as Billy and I were playing catch in my yard, Billy's brother came running up to us and told him he needed to come home right away. No explanation.

I never saw Billy again. Later, I found out his family had moved away.

Many years later, I was a college student at home on break. I was at a gas station when I ran into Billy's brother. We got to talking, and I asked him how Billy and the rest of the family were. He replied, "Good. We have been good ever since my dad was killed."

What I never knew until this moment was that Billy's dad was an abusive drunk. His end came when he went to work, angry and inebriated, and started a confrontation that led to the police shooting and killing him.

Billy's brother said that homelife with their father was a horror. The father would regularly beat his wife and kids, and Billy got the worst of it.

At that moment, as an adult, years removed from the days of bullying, I finally understood I was not responsible for Billy's behavior toward me. I did nothing wrong. I hadn't invited the abuse. The poor kid was silently hurting, badly, and he didn't know what to do other than share the pain.

You may think your story isn't "big" enough for a speech. If you do, you are mistaken.

Take Greg's story about Billy and his bullying. That is not a unique tale. Unique means "one of a kind," and this kind of thing has happened to millions of people in very similar fashion.

What makes it unique is Greg's perspective. That is his own. No one can copy it.

And it's powerful because it features a resolution—a lesson learned from the difficulties—that makes the tale meaningful to others. We can all relate to the idea that we truly don't know the depths of trouble those around us may be experiencing.

Greg has used this story in speeches, and it works. People can relate to it and find value in Greg's particular take on it.

It's not a matter of *if* the personal story is important or big enough, but is it honest and something you feel you must share?

For all the bluster about Americans being a cocky breed, we tend to hide our light. We can be unnecessarily modest. To borrow a British phrase, we don't want to be the "tall poppy." Those are the ones that get chopped down first.

Ignore all that. If it's important to you, it will absolutely be of value to someone in the audience.

One important side note for managing your personal story. Yes, it's important to be vulnerable. Later, you'll see how we also are big fans of sharing and learning from failure and of sharing emotion. All of it makes your story relatable and irresistible.

Please be careful with this. Avoid oversharing. All of that deep feeling and vulnerability is public speaking magic...as long as you have personally resolved all the related issues in your life. Don't talk about issues that are still raw. This is public speaking, not public therapy. We truly don't want to compound the pain in your life by encouraging you to share anything you are not ready to. We would say "share nothing you are not comfortable sharing," but that's not the proper criterion. It's always going to be uncomfortable sharing failure and emotion, and good speakers will get out of their comfort zone.

What we're talking about here is closure or resolution. If the events in question are safely tucked away in your past and you have fully come to grips with it all...then share it with your audience. Please make sure you don't dump unresolved pain on your audience. It's not fair to them, and it accomplishes nothing.

Are you familiar with "hot letters"? It's the idea that when you are really upset by someone, you write a letter explaining all the reasons you're angry. Don't hold back.

Then you stick it in a drawer for a while—a few hours, a few days...whatever it takes to gain perspective of it all. When you retrieve that letter, and if you decide to even send it, there's a good chance you'll give it some heavy editing beforehand.

You can use the same strategy when unsure if you should share something personal in your story. Write it out, let it sit, and come back to it.

Don't worry about losing the moment. You can always give a new speech in the future when you feel the time is right.

DON'T BE A PERFORMER

If you are not a singer or actor, then you're not a performer. Public speakers aren't performers, though it is easy to see why they are perceived to be. The great ones deliver moving speeches full of feeling. Speakers do this knowing they want their time on stage to be clean and professional. And, oh yeah, you're on a stage with a microphone like a stand-up comedian. It sure looks and feels like a performance.

It's not a performance; it's an experience. You are creating an experience where those you wish to communicate with can take away the lion's share of your message and become motivated to respond to it.

Performances are transitory. They are entertaining interludes in our lives that come and go, like eating cotton candy at the fair. There is no permanence of mission. We can love an actor's work and remember it for years without it being any more than a memory. We don't change our lives because of it. We don't do anything differently day-to-day because of it. We just like it.

The experience that follows a great speech should be life-changing. It should challenge the audience member to reexamine what they believe and think. It should also motivate the listener to take specific actions in the future, and all of those actions should become permanent parts of that person's new life.

Plus, that performance can fail. It can fall flat. Be unentertaining.

Your speech experience can be imperfect, peppered with speaking mistakes or other faulty performance issues, and still be of incredible value. When the right mission is backed by passion and a willingness to share, you cannot fail. You will change the world, if only a bit.

Pros know this. They always respect the experience and relegate any performance concerns to the background.

Know what they don't do? Pro speakers don't live or die by feedback. They are so assured by their purpose and message that they simply don't need feedback after the speech. There's no need for validation of what they already know to be honest and true.

CHAPTER 8

EMOTIONAL CONTENT

"Information leads to analysis but emotion leads to action."
—ANDY MASLEN, *PERSUASIVE COPYWRITING: USING PSYCHOLOGY TO ENGAGE, INFLUENCE AND SELL*

ALL OF US HAVE AN EMOTIONAL SIDE AND A RATIONAL side. Two sides of the same coin or, in our cases, our brains. No matter your background, education level, or intent, your emotional side is stronger than your rational side.

How can we make such a statement? Because neuroscientists understand that the subconscious mind handles far more of our day-to-day lives than our conscious mind does. While our conscious mind can translate input and information in words and other formats given to rational scrutiny, our subconscious—juggling way more information in much less time—must use the shorthand of emotion to process it all. That's why you sometimes have a "gut feeling" you can't explain in words. Your subconscious has processed the information and identified a problem while your conscious mind is still catching up. This is universal for all people.

Knowing this is helpful for speechmaking. It identifies common ground for us all because we all react to emotion. Emotional content needs to be part of your personal story in the same way a space-bound vessel needs a booster rocket. The primary and booster rockets independently provide power. Together, you get incredible lift.

Some speakers avoid expressing emotion (similarly to those who struggle with vulnerability). Somehow, we got the message that rationality is preferable to emotionality.

Why should this be? Feeling something precedes achievement. Emotion is close kin to passion. Both are strong motivators. They are the forces that push you to achieve more than reason deems possible.

Plus, because it's a universal force, tapping into it allows you to connect with an audience differently and at a much deeper level.

A STORY FROM VINCE

I was sitting in a barber's chair, getting my bimonthly trim, when the first plane hit the World Trade Center. The TVs in the barbershop were tuned to the *Today* show, and I watched the anchors scrambling to make sense of the breaking news. Then the second plane hit. That was when I told the barber to stop where he was. I grabbed my coat and headed for my TV station to begin a very long day of covering the September 11 attacks.

From my station in Youngstown, Ohio, I had the benefit of distance. Our reporting was gut-wrenching to be sure, but most of us were comfortably far away from the devastation in New York, Washington, and Shanksville, Pennsylvania, and none of our crew personally knew anyone at the impact sites. So our hearts were heavy with only the empathy of observers.

That was on a Tuesday. We spent the rest of the week solely focused on the aftermath.

On Friday and Saturday, my station hosted a telethon, collecting water, food, and other essentials for the survivors in New York City. We planned to drive out to the Javits Center on the west side of Manhattan—which was serving as a supply depot and resource center for the city—and then head to Ground Zero to do some reporting for our viewers in Youngstown.

Everything started out normally enough. The supply drop-off was easy, and the organizers seemed genuinely appreciative of our viewers' generosity.

Then we headed to Ground Zero.

Getting there was tough. Traffic, as you would imagine, was a complete mess, even by New York standards.

On Monday, we got about five blocks from the scene. The rubble burned relentlessly, emitting black smoke into the sky.

That scene was awful enough. Worse was the sight of dust-covered, ragged, and exhausted workers walking away from the debris field while clean, fresh workers marched toward it. There were steady lines of both, moving in opposite directions.

The sheer scope of it, as well as the horrified look on the returning workers' faces, knotted up my stomach. I took deep breaths while reminding myself, "You're a professional. Keep it together."

That worked for a while, until we moved to Washington Square.

People were gathering there to pray, to comfort each other, and to hang up posters, desperately looking for lost loved ones. This was early enough after the attack that some people hoped their friend or family member was just lost, not dead.

The signs were everywhere. The sight was truly overwhelming. For a moment, I could not breathe. When my air did return, I tried interviewing people for my news story. I thought they would reject me for being a vulture, preying on the misery of others. Instead, they welcomed me into their community of suffering and shared their heartfelt, awful stories with me. They seemed to feel a bit better for sharing them, like a mini catharsis. And I was glad they got some small measure of relief.

But I didn't feel better. I felt sick and despondent. I started crying. Not sobbing, mind you, because I still had the benefit of not being personally touched by this tragedy. I felt like I didn't have the right to sob; I hadn't earned it. But the pain in that park was smothering, and I couldn't help but cry. And I kept crying for an hour. (I am crying now as I type this. Just the memory of it still wrecks me.)

My crew tried to get me to rally. They wanted me to shoot my "stand-up"; that's the part of a television news report where the reporter appears on camera. It's important for letting viewers identify the voice they have been hearing during the story (you know, form a connection to the person) and for establishing that the reporter was truly on the scene, doing his job...for you.

I just didn't have it in me. I couldn't stop the tears. So I told the guys there would be no stand-up. And when I put the story together back at my station in Youngstown early the next day, I explained why I wasn't on camera in the actual story for the benefit of the viewers listening.

Later, it was that line about being too broken up to shoot a lousy stand-up that people seemed to connect with.

Speaking effectively is not only about delivering your message with clarity and coherence, but also about engaging your audience on an emotional level.

Greg's friend, mentor, and voice coach, Roger Love, writes in his book *Set Your Voice Free* that the difference between speaking and speaking well (our goal here) is the difference between communicating your ideas and making your listeners feel your ideas.

Reflect on that for a moment. You can make people feel your ideas, and that is immeasurably powerful.

To create this emotional connection between yourself and others, you need to masterfully use your voice and body movements to impart the emotions you want...leaving them feeling the way you want them to feel.

Roger Love teaches that melody is important for engaging your audience (imagine any song that moved you deeply and you'll understand immediately). Love says "Melody is the ultimate way to create an emotional connection with your audience. The right melody can communicate love, hope, excitement or any other emotion you want to convey."[13] Love also says we should pay close attention to the additional components of voice: pitch, pace, tone, and volume. These musical qualities sharpen the delivery of your intended emotions. These musical qualities all give speeches lift. Your words will become memorable and powerful.

Here, we'll spend a little time exploring how to expand your emotional range to capture the ear, eye, and spirit of your audience.

Neurolinguistic programming (NLP) and hypnotherapy techniques developed by Dr. Richard Bandler and Milton Erickson can be helpful with your mastery of emotional range. So, too, can an article by Assael Romanelli, PhD, entitled "What's Your Emotional Range?" We hope our book (this book) is just the start of your ongoing studies.

REFRAME YOUR EMOTIONS

NLP teaches that our emotions are largely determined by thought patterns. To expand your emotional range, you can learn to reframe your thoughts and emotions in a more positive or constructive light. For example, instead of feeling anxious about a new experience, you can reframe it as excitement and anticipation. This technique can help you effectively shift your perspective, experiencing a wider, richer range of emotions.

Romanelli suggests that developing a wider emotional range involves learning to identify and express that range of feelings even if that exploration is uncomfortable (at first). Actually, it most likely will be uncomfortable. We've learned all too well how to cover emotions, not express them. Still, if you struggle with this, you will become more emotionally intelligent and resilient.

---

[13] "Learning Center," Roger Love, accessed September 4, 2024, https://rogerlove.com/learning-center-v2/; Roger Love, direct communication with the author.

USE LANGUAGE TO EXPAND YOUR EMOTIONAL VOCABULARY

The words we use shape our emotional experiences. By expanding your emotional vocabulary and using more descriptive language to express it, you deepen your emotional range. For example, instead of saying you are "happy," you can say you're "elated" or "ecstatic." Using more specific language directly accesses those varied emotions, the ones previously hidden or avoided.

CHALLENGE YOUR ASSUMPTIONS

Romanelli writes that challenging assumptions about your emotions can help you break out of old and powerful (and limiting) patterns and develop greater emotional range. By being open to experiencing new feelings, you can expand your emotional experiences and increase your emotional intelligence.

MODEL EMOTIONS

NLP also suggests we can learn from others by modeling their behavior and thought patterns. To expand your emotional range, you can observe people who embody the emotions you want to experience and then try to emulate their behavior and thinking. Monkey see, monkey do, if you will.

CHAPTER 9

PRACTICE AND FAIL

YOU HAVE LIKELY DONE NOTHING LIKE THIS BEFORE. Why would you? Most people don't pay such close attention to the calibration and delivery of emotional content. Therefore, because it is new, developing emotional range will require practice and persistence. Try incorporating these strategies into your daily life and interactions with others. Give yourself permission to feel and express a wider range of emotions. Over time, you'll become more comfortable and adept at using your emotions to connect with others and create powerful experiences.

EMBRACING FAILURE

We love this particular thought from Bill Gates: "Success is a lousy teacher."[14] If you follow everything we tell you to do in this book and try your hardest to do it correctly, and put your heart and soul into it, you're going to fail sometimes. Eventually—and we can't tell

---

14 Bill Gates, *The Road Ahead* (New York: Viking, 1995), 35.

you when or why—at some point, you will succeed beyond your boldest expectations. But you're going to fail quite a bit before then.

No doubt you've heard other thinkers advise that "if you're not failing, you're not trying" or that "we learn through failure." Both statements are absolutely true, though knowing that doesn't make it any easier.

On the second point—learning through failure—you should know you learn through failure *if* you take the time to reflect on that experience, recalibrate either your thinking or actions, and then try again and again until you succeed.

Thomas Edison, one of history's great inventors, had a thousand unsuccessful attempts in creating the light bulb. When a reporter asked him, "How does it feel to fail a thousand times?" He responded, "I didn't fail a thousand times. The light bulb was an invention with a thousand steps."

A more contemporary inventor, James Dyson, creator of the very popular Dyson vacuum cleaner, attempted 5,126 prototypes over the course of five years and racked up $10,000 in debt before he produced a winner.

J. K. Rowling of *Harry Potter* fame was a depressed single mother on welfare when she wrote her first book, which was rejected by twelve different publishers before it was picked up.

The great master Picasso produced 13,500 paintings in his lifetime. Only a handful of those are masterpieces.

We could go on. The web and Hollywood are bursting at the seams with failure-to-success stories. They register with us and motivate us. Who didn't smile and maybe cheer a little watching the movie *Rudy* and seeing our undersized, marginally talented hero get into the game he loved after years of single-minded dedication and lots of bruises?

Once a person realizes they truly gain valuable knowledge through failure, they actually look forward to failing. They find joy in it because they know their breakthrough is closer than it ever has been.

Great speakers are not exempt. They fail, and they learn from it.

A STORY FROM GREG

Some years ago, when my son, Brad, was in Little League, I got inspired. At the time, we were paying pitching coaches to work with Brad. It was a major time commitment for everyone involved. We logged hundreds of hours together: Brad, me, and the coaches.

Soon, all that work began to reveal a big idea. We could develop a training aid for pitchers, a specially designed glove that helps train the player with proper throwing mechanics. This was the birth of our product—Strike-Out Strippz.

What followed was a rush. We got our patents, went into production, and best of all, negotiated our way onto the shelves of Dick's Sporting Goods stores in our region. Then, on top of all that initial success, we signed up a top-tier spokesman—eleven-time All-Star, two-time World Series champ, and seven-time Cy Young Award winner Roger Clemens. We were on our way.

Until 2007 and the Mitchell Report.

Former US senator George Mitchell completed a nearly two-year investigation into the use of steroids and human growth hormone in Major League Baseball. Eighty-eight players in all were (allegedly) taking the banned substances, including our guy, Roger Clemens.

In what seemed like hours, Strike-Out Strippz were pulled from the shelves and our business died. That's part one of my failure.

Part two came a few weeks later, when I realized I had to come up with the money to cover our losses. (And before you say, "Greg, why not declare bankruptcy and walk away?" believe me, I thought about it. I just couldn't do it. I owe, so I pay.)

I did it. I really didn't have much of a choice. Over a long period of time, I made everyone whole again. It required painful sacrifice, but I managed to overcome the failure of my business/passion project.

Still, this unfortunate episode taught me valuable lessons about partnering, business, and life. Looking back, I can honestly say it was a big lesson that yielded even bigger benefits. Instead of letting this failure ruin me or define me, I found a way to learn from it, and my businesses today have become better for it.

As Gates says, "Success is a lousy teacher." We learn by doing, and doing sometimes (often?) means failing.

If you're not failing as you learn, you simply aren't taking any chances. You're not pushing yourself. Instead, you're taking the conservative path you've walked a thousand times before. You already know everything on that path. There's nothing more to learn there.

Keep failure and success close together. They belong with each other.

"Grit is that 'extra something' that separates the most successful people from the rest. It's the passion, perseverance and stamina that we must channel in order to stick with our dreams until they become reality."

—TRAVIS BRADBERRY, AMERICAN AUTHOR

If a genie were to appear and ask if you wanted the gift of talent or of grit, many of you would opt for talent. That's the simple choice. Talent feels natural, while grit signals there's work ahead. Even the name "grit" is tough, conjuring up images of dusty cowboys or sooty factory workers sweating through a marathon of work, trying to get the job done.

The problem is talent only gets you so far. There are plenty of people in the world who have a natural talent (or aptitude, if you prefer) for something yet never truly excel in it. Without dedication and deliberate practice (more on this later), that talent peters out. It becomes unrealized potential.

The person with grit, on the other hand, finds a way to get it done. They may not have the natural talent that makes it look easy, and they may take longer getting to the finish line, but they achieve. And over time, the gritty individual will achieve more—much more—than the simply talented individual.

If your life's purpose points you in a particular direction, and you don't seem to have any initial talent for pursuing that direction, go anyway. Put your head down, get to work, and don't let the bumps along the way push you off the path. You'll get there. Greg is not the only person who powered his way toward excellence in public speaking. You can do it too.

CHAPTER 10

VOICE

"How wonderful is the human voice! It is indeed the organ of the soul. The intellect of man is enthroned visibly on his forehead and in his eye, and the heart of man is written on his countenance, but the soul, the soul reveals itself in the voice only."

—HENRY WADSWORTH LONGFELLOW, AMERICAN POET

"VOICE" MEANS MORE THAN ONE THING IN TODAY'S LANguage. There are those who want to "make their voice heard." They are the advocates, the champions of a cause. For them, "voice" is more about the message than the actual sound. We all have a "voice" that we wish to be heard, and we have tried to address those issues—identifying what you stand for, clarifying your values, finding the correct vehicles for your messages through emotional storytelling, and creating compelling content—in other sections of this book.

Here, we want to address your actual voice—the sound that emanates from your body, forms words and sentences, and articulates thought. This is an examination of your literal voice.

To be clear, this is not a cosmetic or superficial concern. Please don't be fooled into thinking that only the message matters. If you must place a hierarchy of value on the two, you're free to do that on your own time. We feel they are of equal importance.

Imagine walking up to a person you have never met before. You will, as all people do, form opinions about and expectations of that person based on what you see. That's your first data input. Perhaps you'll combine that with the setting you are in, giving those visual clues some context.

So, you're at a professional conference, let's say, and you spot a person you want to speak with. He's well dressed, tall, athletically built, and handsome. Can you see him in your mind?

Now imagine that, as he introduces himself to you, he speaks in a high-pitched, squeaky voice. These things don't match at all. You will be confused as your brain tries to reconcile the mismatch. And unless you quickly discover another reason for interaction, you will likely be repulsed. The meeting will be over. You'll search for a reason to break off and find another person to talk to.

Voice matters. In all human interactions, we try our best to be attractive to others. Not only sexually but socially and intellectually as well. Our need to bond with others is strong, the product of hundreds of years of instinctive learning. Our ancestors needed to attract others to form communities for mutual protection and survival. Fighting, hunting, farming, and child-rearing together was the only way to live well then, and we carry the need to attract now.

Which is why speakers must work on making their voices as appealing as possible.

This is achievable.

A STORY FROM VINCE

When I was searching for a purpose (which I thought of as a "career" back then—I was too young to know the two things are different, though often connected, if you're lucky), I stumbled into television news. I had gone to graduate school to pursue communications with no real plan for how I would use it.

Fortunately, I met Dr. Marsha Della-Giustina, the director of Emerson College's journalism program. I heard Marsha speak at the grad student orientation, and I immediately wanted to take classes with her. Marsha was an openly enthusiastic woman whose energy and love of journalism was infectious. She was also a barrier breaker: the first female news producer in the Boston television market, multiple Emmy Award winner, and she boasted a doctorate from Boston University. She was the complete package—a pro's pro who loved to teach her craft, and several of my fellow students and I formed a quasi-cult around her. I was even fortunate enough to serve as Marsha's grad assistant for a time.

After two years studying all Marsha gave me, I was ready to take to the airwaves. Would I become the next Peter Jennings or Dan Rather or Bryant Gumbel? Why not? I was the product of an excellent journalism program; I was reasonably bright, super curious, and highly driven; and, back then, I was a thin, handsome young man. What more do you need to succeed in TV news?

Well, you need a voice. And I didn't have it.

I would tape our student newscasts at school and bring them home for my girlfriend at the time, now my wife, Laurie. She and the rest of our families would watch them and offer support because that's what loved ones do.

Except they never pointed out that I had an awful voice. It was airy and higher pitched than it should have been, and it certainly did not fit my physical self at all. I was so busy trying to learn how to be a journalist that I never took proper stock of my vocal deficits, but Laurie did. Secretly. It wasn't until years later that she shared with me her fear that I would never get a job in broadcasting because my on-air voice was so bad. (Side note: While my speaking voice wasn't great, it was better than my "on air" voice. In retrospect, I realized I was doing all the wrong things when speaking for broadcast and tightening my musculature up to the point that it was ruining my voice. My regular speaking voice allowed others to think I might be OK eventually. After all, my voice wasn't terrible all the time.)

There is no doubt in my mind that my initial vocal shortcomings limited my career advancement in the early days. Fortunately for me, I earned my first TV news jobs through hard work and connections. And I found new mentors to finish the work Marsha had done. They showed me how to optimize my voice. I never tried to "Ted Baxter" my voice on the air, making it artificially and ridiculously low. Instead, I learned how to relax and support my voice properly with breath. If you listen to my old tapes (which I will never play for you...too embarrassing) and hear me now, there is a two- to three-octave difference in pitch.

I still don't sound like Jennings or Tom Brokaw or any of the other deep, rumbling voices popular in my journalism days, but I wish I had then the voice I have now.

"The human voice is the most perfect instrument of all."
—ARVO PÄRT, ESTONIAN COMPOSER

We quote a musician here because it's important you think of your body as a musical instrument and your voice as music.

Can't sing yet? Don't worry about it. You can still make your speaking voice a tool for capturing attention and motivating others. You just have to understand how it works.

Your body is an instrument that produces sounds. It begins with the air in your lungs that you push through your trachea (windpipe) to your larynx and then vocal cords, which vibrate and create sound waves. From there, the sound waves move from the vocal cords to your mouth (and sinus cavity), where your soft palate, tongue, and jaw move to shape and articulate the sounds. Also, the areas and amount of tension you are holding in your body directly affect the resonance of your voice. For example, if you hold excess tension in your chest, the resonance of your voice will be thin and heady.

If we were talking about a guitar, we would have a similar process: right-hand fingers strum or pick the strings, which vibrate, left-hand fingers press on the strings at different intervals to change the vibration, and the sound fills the void of the sound hole (in an acoustic guitar, anyway), where it resonates as it spills out into the air to be heard.

Just like musical instruments, voice production involves physical mechanics. There's movement of the apparatus, which results in movement of the air, which is the very essence of sound.

And, as with musical instruments, a body that is tuned for performance produces better sound. This certainly could involve physical fitness because, typically, an athlete comes to understand the musculature of their body and, as a result, can manipulate their body for the sake of performance. You do not, however, have to be an athlete to become a great speaker. You just need to be aware of the muscles at play in the speaking process and learn to use them... no running or jumping involved. It's learning how to play your instrument.

The voice itself has the properties of music, which are:

- Pitch
- Tone
- Melody
- Volume
- Pace (including pauses)

Find a great TED speech on YouTube—like those by Sir Ken Robinson, Brené Brown, Simon Sinek, and of course, for fun, Tom Thum—and watch for these elements. You'll hear speakers adjust their pitch to fit the mood they are creating. They will adopt distinct tones to match the subject, and they will speed up or slow down or get louder or softer, all for effect.

Now find a speech in a language you do not understand and listen. You won't know the words, but you will note the melodies of the spoken word. Also, you will probably understand what feeling the speaker is conveying because music is universal. You'll simply feel the meaning, much like you do with a pop song with garbled lyrics you can't understand.

As important and unique as human voices are, you won't have your voice "as is" for too long. Our voices mature. You've probably had the experience of talking to an older person and hearing a surprisingly smooth and rich voice. We've even coined phrases for some of these sounds: whiskey cured, smoked cured, etc. The truth of the matter is, even if you do not smoke or drink, your voice will change and become truly "mature" around fifty years of age. If you're there already, great. Enjoy it. If not, you have something to look forward to.

VOCAL DYNAMICS

Music is not the repetition of the same sound, at the same volume, and in the same tempo. Neither is higher-level public speaking. Your speaking voice has all the elements of music at its disposal. You should use them.

Vocal dynamics involve using the range of changes available to you.

Not arbitrarily. You should not speak more loudly or more quickly for any reason. If your vocal choices don't match your content, they will be jarring to hear. This is just as poor a choice as adopting a boring, monotone delivery.

Singers practice vocal dynamics that serve their songs, and speakers should do the same thing. As you rehearse a speech, try changing its pitch, tone, melody, volume, and pace (including pauses). Get rid of the changes that don't work and note the ones that do. Building a little diversity of sound into your presentation will make it far more exciting and memorable for those who hear it.

It's all about vocal flexibility and adapting your sound to the environment, audience, and content of your speech. Adjusting your voice strategically is a great way to connect with people and make them feel comfortable with you.

ACHIEVING YOUR BEST VOICE

The next time you wake up from a good night's sleep, spend a moment talking to yourself. Record it on your phone, if you can, and watch it back. Chances are pretty good your morning voice will be the best voice you speak with all day.

Here's why. When you first rouse from sleep, your body is still relaxed. The expectations and tension of the day haven't had a chance to tense your muscles, and it's during this phase of maximum relaxation that your best voice emerges.

Relaxed voices are lower in pitch, and they are usually fuller. Your relaxed body is enabling the vibrations from your vocal cords to resonate unrestricted within the cavities of your body: chest, head, and nose. For men and women both, this is your optimum resonant voice.

If you've been paying attention, you've picked up on the two keys here—relaxation and vibration. And now that you know what the goal should be, how do you achieve it when awake? You train; that's how.

Except for charley horses or other muscle spasms, where your body is in mutiny and the remedies require either time or medicine, you can make your body relax. We admit, it's a strange concept. Most people feel if they truly could relax on command, they'd do it all the time.

There are times when your body tenses for your best interest. If there's a threat—real or perceived—your mind and body know they need to prepare to defend you. That is not what we're talking about here.

In speaker prep, you can take time to become quiet. Get rid of the distractions of the world around you and become mindful of your body. Listen to your breath. Now, think about the various parts of your body and focus on releasing tension. Pay attention to how the release feels. Repeat this process with other parts of your body, starting with the top of your head, then forehead, then jaw, then the back of your tongue, then your throat, neck, shoulders, chest—continue until you reach your toes. You'll find you can achieve a Zen state, something meditative. After all, your brain controls your muscles, and you can prompt your brain to issue those release commands.

This, of course, is in the perfect environment. Without noise, stress, and distractions, it's fairly simple to release all tension.

The key to on-command relaxation when you need it, distractions and all, is to practice the relaxation exercise above regularly. Soon, your body and brain will build little shortcuts that help you achieve your desired relaxed state more quickly. You may also find it helpful to create a mantra or routine that you incorporate into your relaxation practice. These can serve as cues for your body, making for quicker and more efficient vocal relaxation. The more you practice, the better you will become at it. The process will eventually become strong enough to endure the rigors of daily living.

Try it. You'll be happier with the voice that follows.

You can also practice vibration. Without using too much force, which could damage your vocal cords, practice low humming for a few minutes every day. Find the lowest tone you can achieve smoothly and without the sound breaking and hum in that tone. You can do it to a tune if you like, or just hum in intervals. It doesn't really matter. The point of the exercise is allowing your cords to vibrate freely. And as with the relaxation exercise, where repeated practice builds pathways to get to the goal faster and amid distractions, you'll develop the same consistency with vibration.

Here's an exercise you may find helpful: feel your Adam's apple with your fingers, then hum in lower and lower tones until you sense your Adam's apple drop. Then stop. That point and that tone are your natural "bottom register." That's the lowest vibration point you can manage comfortably; anything lower will sound artificial and could be harmful to your vocal cords.

Now, once you've found the bottom, hum again while touching your Adam's apple and raise your tone until you sense the Adam's apple rise. Stop. That's the top of your register. This optimal vibration range varies for everyone, so don't let others' tones influence you and what you can achieve. Respect your range and trust us. That range is enough for you to be an excellent speaker.

Everybody appreciates a full, resonant voice. It's a voice that commands respect, exudes authority, and frankly, is easier to understand than some higher-pitched voices. You can maximize your voice toward the ideal. What you should never do is try to adopt an artificial voice. As we said, your body is an instrument. Certain notes are simply never meant to be played by some instruments. A violin does not have the depth of sound that a bass does. Soprano and baritone saxophones differ significantly.

Respect those differences. If you have a higher pitch, make it as rich as you can and stop. You can't be an authentic speaker with a phony voice. Besides, the world is better with variety. You can—and should—have a distinct voice.

PAUSING...AND WHY IT'S MORE THAN THE ABSENCE OF VOICE

Pausing is a powerful tool in speech delivery.

1. Gives Time to Think: Pausing allows you to gather your thoughts and choose the following words after "listening" to the audience after a phrase.
2. Enhances Comprehension: It gives your audience time to digest and understand what's been said, allowing the message to resonate more deeply.
3. Adds Emphasis: A well-timed pause can emphasize a particular point, making it more memorable.
4. Controls Pace: Pausing can help control the rhythm and tempo of your speech, ensuring it doesn't feel rushed or monotonous.
5. Improves Articulation: Pausing can prevent you from stumbling over words or getting tongue-tied.
6. Reduces Fillers: Instead of using "um," "uh," or other filler words, pausing can create a cleaner and more polished presentation.
7. Engages Audience: A pause can create suspense or intrigue, capturing your audience's attention and keeping them engaged.

8. Conveys Confidence: Pausing can show that you are confident in your message and not afraid of silence.
9. Allows for Breath: On a practical level, pausing lets you breathe, which can be vital in maintaining a strong voice.
10. Facilitates Interaction: A pause can create space for your audience to have questions or reactions in interactive settings.
11. Promotes Connection and Presence: A pause creates a moment of stillness, allowing you and your audience to be genuinely present. This shared experience fosters a more profound connection, reminding everyone involved of the human element and shared understanding of communication. In the silence, there's a mutual acknowledgment, a shared breath, and an unspoken bond that strengthens the message and its reception.

Incorporating strategic pauses can make your speech more effective, memorable, and engaging. It's a subtle skill that can vastly improve your public-speaking abilities with practice.

PART 3

THE PLAN

"Never be afraid to raise your voice for honesty and truth and compassion against injustice and lying and greed. If people all over the world... would do this, it would change the earth."
—WILLIAM FAULKNER, AMERICAN WRITER

YOUR FOUNDATION IS IN PLACE. YOU HAVE AND—MORE importantly—understand your purpose for public speaking, and you now know how to power your effort. You're ready to make a big impact on your organization, your community...even the world at large. This is your moment, and we know from personal experience this is a very exciting time, an anticipatory moment like the seconds before the stall gates lift at the Kentucky Derby or the green light flashes, letting NASCAR drivers know it's time to *go*.

Well, hold on there for a moment. *You* may be ready, but what about your talk? Sure, you're full of passion. Your message and mission are very personal to you, perhaps to where you no longer see the separation between you and it. That's natural. It's also a trap. That's because a talk with no preparation is an invitation for disaster.

How do you optimize this moment? How do you ensure your message is compelling and well received? How do you deliver it like a pro? How do you create an event that lives in the minds of your audience long after it's over?

You need a plan. And we'll be honest with you right up front—your plan requires work. This is no time to be lazy or excessively confident in your charms as an off-the-cuff speaker. By now, you have already invested time and energy into figuring out what you are a champion for—what you're willing to sacrifice and fight for—and what will give your campaign life and energy. It would be a shame to waste all that effort on an ill-conceived talk.

Let's get to work. Don't worry; it's not like researching and writing the term paper you loathed doing back in your student days. Now you'll work on something you care about. Here, preparation becomes action steps toward *your* goals, *your* vision. We've all heard the expression "if you love what you do, you'll never work a day in your life," and we all know that's nonsense. Often, you work even harder at what you love, and you just don't mind it. Try to imagine something more rewarding, more satisfying, and more exciting than working diligently on something you truly care about that creates meaningful, positive change. It's hard to visualize, isn't it?

Alright then. Let's get to work.

CHAPTER 11

WHAT'S THE PLAN?

WE'RE NOT BIG ON COOKIE-CUTTER APPROACHES TO anything. Speeches are deeply personal, and your speaker prep will probably reflect that. We do, however, know that creating a pro-level talk always involves attending to the following:

- Content creation
- Voice
- Breath
- Body movement
- On-camera strategies
- Stage fright management

To be clear, we should point out that nothing on this list is inherently more important than another. You may experience some deficits in one or more particular aspects, which would make focus on those areas feel more pressing. As always, go with your gut. Still, it needs to be said that everything on this list is vital. It's all part of a good plan. And giving insufficient attention to any of those elements will weaken the final product. Therefore, we're going to spend some time on each aspect. We urge you to do the same.

CONTENT

I know we just said that all of your plan's elements are important, and they are. That said, if you were to rank each plan element in terms of importance (not that you need to, but if you had to), then content would be last on the list.

So why is it first in this chapter?

Because (a) it still matters—a lot, in fact; and (b) it is the area where many speakers get hung up and lost. Have you ever experienced the sheer terror of approaching the day of your talk and still figuring out "What am I going to say?" Less experienced speakers can become paralyzed by the self-imposed demands of figuring out *the words*.

Words matter. Think back to how American presidential addresses endure as part of the culture—Kennedy's "Ask not what your country can do for you, but what you can do for your country"; Roosevelt's "The only thing we have to fear…is fear itself"; Lincoln's "Fourscore and seven years ago our fathers brought forth, on this continent, a new nation, conceived in liberty, and dedicated to the proposition that all men are created equal."

Well-crafted words evoke powerful feelings in those who hear them.

And here's another well-written quote that puts it all in perspective: politician Carl W. Buehner's "They may forget what you said—but they will never forget how you made them feel."[15]

When it's all said and done, your audience will not be able to recite your entire talk word for word. Hopefully, they remember a

---

[15] Richard L. Evans, *Richard Evans' Quote Book* (Salt Lake City, UT: Publishers Press, 1971), 244.

quote or two. Ideally, they will remember your mission, perspective, and call to action. What must happen, though, is that you have to make them feel something. The actual "what" of that depends on you: it can be happy, excited, motivated, sad, angry...whatever. The specifics are up to you. What matters is that you make them feel something strongly enough to change their thinking or perspective.

BEGIN AT THE END

Target identified. You know you want your audience to feel something you inspired when you leave the stage. Excellent! You've just completed the most important "to-do" item on your content creation checklist. You must know your final destination before you begin the journey. You must begin at the end.

This may sound counterintuitive. In school, our teachers taught us that all stories have a beginning, middle, and end, and many of us assumed we had to create content at the beginning. That's like going to the airport and picking your vacation destination by looking at the departures board. If you don't know where you're going, how do you know what to pack? You could have shorts and bathing suits in your bag as you buy your ticket to Alaska in December. That's terrible planning.

Now, before you accuse us of not being spontaneous or lacking the spirit of adventure, consider this: of all the blockbuster movies you've enjoyed over the years—think *The Godfather*, *Star Wars*, *Top Gun*, *The Wizard of Oz*, and the like—how many of them do you suppose the filmmakers wrote scripts for *without* having the ending in mind? We can assure you, not a single one. Why would a studio invest millions of dollars into a production without first knowing it was going to end with a big, emotional bang? You have to know what's in the last act before you write act one. Otherwise, you can't build to the big moment.

That's what your speeches need to do: build to the climax. By the way, this reverse-engineering approach will end up helping you. Now, during the content creation phase, you can use your ending as a target. You should include anything and everything that serves that ending—whatever builds your talk and moves it toward that clearly defined goal. Conversely, everything not targeted toward the ending you want needs to go. Throw it out. It doesn't matter if the wording is clever or if you personally enjoy recalling that tangent. It has to go. Successful speeches are like great poetry; they are dense with feeling and only as long as they need to be thanks to the writer's appreciation of word economy. Keep it short, punchy, and on target...always.

The intelligence of your audience is another factor weighing in favor of beginning with the end. Speakers never underestimate their audiences. People come to a talk (hopefully) open to new ideas, tempered with their native common sense. Some people refer to it as a BS meter. We all instinctively know garbage when we hear it. Our conscious minds might be fooled for a while, yet our subconscious usually knows when something is wrong. Your gut tells you when something is "off." And we believe that if you do not prepare your content properly, planning your ending and building toward it, your audience will feel the one thing you never want them to: disconnected. At some level, they may even resent that you came to them with an unorganized thought in the guise of a poorly planned speech. Respecting your audience means giving them the organization they crave.

Does that strike you as odd? That people crave organization? They do. Think back to a large group activity, personal or professional. Didn't you get more out of it when everyone's role in that activity was clearly defined? And do you remember the stress and anxiety you felt when you were left to figure it out on your own, with no idea if your assessment was right or wrong? Audiences want a guided tour. They don't want to wander around, searching for meaning in your disorganized talk. You do them a favor when you present an organized talk. They will connect with the content, engage with you, be grateful for the clarity, and remember how you made them feel. If you leave them to their own devices, they will feel things you never intended, and your time with them will have been wasted.

Want an example? Go to Google and search "Sarah Palin and Iowa Freedom Summit." It's a video from 2015 when the former Alaskan governor and candidate for vice president Sarah Palin spoke at a political event in Iowa, home of America's first-in-the-nation presidential caucus.

During the presidential run in 2008, you may remember Governor Palin had a bunch of tussles with the press. Reporters kept asking her questions about foreign policy, and Palin did not handle them well. She was clearly not well versed in international affairs. She was, however, charming in her way. She had an easy smile and a plain-spoken style that appealed to Republican voters. As a result, many in her base defended her against a seemingly biased press. They felt she was being treated unfairly, which only served to build loyalty among her people. It doesn't matter what you say but how you make them feel, remember?

Fast-forward seven years and the narrative changes. Now Governor Palin has no foil, no opponent to make her look sympathetic. It's just her at the microphone, saying whatever she wants, and it's a train wreck. Apparently, her teleprompter broke, and while she most definitely had a printed version of her speech, she chose to ad-lib big parts of the talk. The speech was a disorganized mess of bizarre and incoherent asides. It was, in a word, weird. This is not a partisan observation. It is fair to say Republicans, Democrats—really anyone—would have the same impression.

If Palin had gone to the podium with a clear ending in mind, she may have stood a chance of ad-libbing a decent speech. Her humor and charm may have helped her get away with any organizational flaws in the talk; audiences are forgiving, after all. However, it is evident that the governor lacked a specific conclusion. She meandered all over the place, finding lines that landed with those watching. She got lost, and, as a result, so did her audience.

This reminds me of the advice Jordan Peterson, thought leader and professor, gives his students: speak on topics that you have ten times more knowledge on than you offer in your talk. This depth will reflect in your delivery and be most beneficial for you and your audience.[16]

Begin at the end with depth of understanding and knowledge of your topic. It's the best assurance of success for content organization and a speech that brings listeners to their feet.

FOCUS AND THE THREE LEGS

A STORY FROM GREG

From the time I was a very young boy, martial arts has always fascinated me. My father, however, did not share my passion. He had no interest in "fighting" and would not let me train in karate until my teens. (By then, what could he do? Boys are much easier to manage than young men.) Now I could get "hands on" with a sport I had only loved from a distance.

My instructor, Dave Buker, told me I had to focus on *one thing* at a time if I hoped to develop any skill. He stressed the need to work on

---

16   Jordan Peterson, "How to Sound Smart When You Talk," Wise Advice Motivation, posted November 17, 2021, YouTube video, 00:08:44, https://www.youtube.com/watch?v=Q_ZeFOO9owM.

one technical skill—one technique—before moving on to another. His mantra became "You focus on one thing at a time." He would explain, "There is no such thing as active multitasking." To which I responded, "But I've seen people multitask."

My teacher looked at me for a moment, then grabbed three balls from the floor of the dojo and said "catch them all" as he flung them at me.

I failed. And to make sure I got the lesson, Dave threw all three balls at me at once several more times. Each time, he instructed me to "catch them all." Of course, I didn't. I'd like to think I have decent athletic abilities, but I know I only have two hands.

This was an effective early lesson in focus. Staying focused enabled me to develop my karate skills, and today I am a sixth-degree black belt. (Which, by definition, makes me a master. Except, as Socrates said, "I know that I know nothing," meaning when you develop expertise in an area, you are likely to have the newfound perspective that you truly have much to learn. In my case, what about all the other martial arts? Sure, I know a lot about one, which shines a bright light on the fact that I still have years of study ahead of me.)

As the expression goes, "How do you eat an elephant? One bite at a time." You, too, may feel there are multitaskers in the world, those with the incredible ability to do so many varied tasks simultaneously. Who wouldn't want to aspire to be one of them?

It took years for us to realize what is really happening behind the scenes. People defined as "multitaskers" are those who have trained their subconscious minds to perform skills they have already mastered while their conscious mind focuses on the difficult tasks. Some refer to this as "unconscious competence." Think about driving, for example. If you've been behind the wheel for years (decades, even), you no longer actively think about putting on seat belts, using turn signals, checking mirrors or blind-spot indicators before changing lanes, or any of the dozens of little jobs one must perform to drive from point A to point B safely.

People sometimes say, "I can do that in my sleep" when talking about doing something simple. What they are really saying is "I have worked on that skill to a point where I now have subconscious competence. I don't have to think about it. I just do it."

Your subconscious mind can manage a lot all at once. Our conscious minds, by comparison, need to focus, usually on one skill or task at a time until we master it. If you make the mistake of spreading your conscious mind out too much to cover multiple skills and tasks, you end up with mediocrity.

By the way, don't make the mistake of equating multitasking with intelligence. You may admire successful people who seem to be multitaskers and come to believe being smart has something to do with it. The reality is even truly intelligent people benefit from focused learning and training. In fact, it's likely their intelligence came from hours spent learning one skill or subject area at a time with dedicated focus. Hard work with deliberate practice and the guidance of an expert is not a compromise made by the less able, but rather an effective strategy for mastering anything you desire.

Like public speaking. Or the topic you are sharing with an audience.

THE TRIPOD

Yes, your speech needs to be focused, the tighter the better. This helps you as the speaker develop something manageable and deliverable. Pick a topic, figure out how you want to leave the audience feeling about it at the end, and start crafting the talk, focusing sharply on both the topic and the targeted finish.

Of course, there are exceptions. Sometimes circumstances call for an "everything but the kitchen sink" talk—a speech that is broad and covers a lot of information. You can do that if you like, but we promise you the audience won't remember much of it.

Picture yourself in Home Depot, looking for the one specific bolt you need to finish your home project. The store is massive. There are shelves rising all the way to the ceiling with everything from lumber to curtains. Without the aisle signs, you would be truly lost in Home Depot. And the signs provide minimal help. Even if you find your section—in this case screws, bolts, and fasteners—you still have a jungle of products to sort through before you find what you came for. It's overwhelming.

And that's how an audience feels after being on the receiving end of an "everything but the kitchen sink" speech—overwhelmed. The problem with comprehensive speeches—those with broader versus narrower focus—is that audience members are so overloaded they cannot find anything to grab on to and internalize. If your goal is to inspire change and motivate others to action, you need to give your audience something they can take with them when they leave the venue and return to their lives. It must be memorable. You do your audience a service when you shine the spotlight on one thing, making it easier to find and remember.

Still, we're sure you're concerned about finding ways to pass the time. You were asked to give, let's say, a twenty-minute speech. How do you spend twenty minutes talking about "one thing"?

Focusing on one thing is a matter of priority. Some call it a hierarchy in the mind. No one expects you to talk about one solitary idea and walk away from the mic. That's a statement, not a speech.

Instead, think of your speech as a tripod. Your big idea—the focus—is the thing on the top. And while that's most important, it can't do much on its own. There still needs to be some context and background. That's where the three legs come in. We have found that three supporting points underpinning the main point work very well. Three is the perfect number to allow for deeper understanding of the topic through explanation, context, and history without bogging down the audience with too much background.

The focus remains because your three supporting points all connect to the central topic sitting on top of the tripod, one apparatus with four discrete parts. Or, if you prefer a more active analogy, think of an arrow. The sharpened metal tip is the main topic, while the shaft, feathers, and bow help to deliver that topic to the target, your audience. The better your supporting elements are, the better your chances of shooting a bull's-eye.

CHAPTER 12

HOW VERSUS WHY

DO YOU WANT TO EDUCATE OR ADVOCATE? IT'S NOT A trick question, and there is no wrong answer. Because, while speeches can be as varied and unique as their creators, there are two types of speeches: informative and persuasive.

It's important to decide which speech type you want to deliver. They are different yet not foreign to each other. You can give an informational speech with a persuasive ending. You may also give a persuasive speech with informational elements in the conclusion. Some people mistakenly believe that informational speeches consist only of facts, while persuasive talks rely solely on emotion. That's not true. There's no law against mixing elements, as long as it serves your mission and message.

That said, you should pick one of these distinct speech types and stick to it to serve yourself well.

With informational speeches, you are the expert who gets to showcase their expertise. You explain *how* a thing came to be and how it works. Informational speeches are linear in their organization and very direct. They often convey thoughts on the steps, items, skills, and beliefs required to accomplish something.

Persuasive speeches are about perspective and passion. These talks offer the audience new ways of experiencing something. They change the way people think and feel in sometimes subtle ways.

Both types are wonderful and can change lives, so don't be afraid to stake a claim on one orientation and begin writing.

Regardless of which type of speech you select, you need to back it up. Speak only about topics/events/philosophies you have either lived through personally or have studied intensely. If you do not know your topic intimately, it's not really your topic. Napoleon Hill wrote *Think and Grow Rich* as a research project, and he did so by (a) researching his subject and (b) declaring where his personal connection to the subject came from. As a result, he earned his large audience of readers.

If you still need some clarity around creating your persuasive or informational speech, here are some templates Greg developed to help you write out your core statement. This is straight from class materials he hands out to his honors communications students at Youngstown State University.

FINDING CORE IDEA, SUPPORTING POINTS, AND ANCHOR WORD

1. To be most effective, your talk should focus on ONE main idea. NO MORE. ONE! What does your audience need to know? (e.g., Everyone could/should WHAT? [WHY] or Everyone can WHAT? [HOW])
2. How is it immediately relevant to your current audience? (***THIS IS VERY IMPORTANT***)
3. What are two to three supporting points?
4. What plural noun (Anchor Word) connects your points so they are parallel?
5. Examples: lessons, points, beliefs, reasons, facts, needs, keys, gifts, norms, truths

ONE SENTENCE

(WHY) Every person can _____ by understanding three important _____. [ANCHOR WORD]

(HOW) Every person should _____ by learning three important _____. [ANCHOR WORD or "reasons"]

EXAMPLES

Two people wrote this book together. We are actual human beings with years of experience in both general communications and pro-level speeches. The following examples were written using ChatGPT. AI is becoming a readily available tool for content creators and we, like many others, are exploring its possibilities. We figured you could use some examples of persuasive and informational speeches, so we asked OpenAI to write them for you. When you come up to Chapter 13, "Words, Words, Words," that is where our original writing resumes.

HERE'S AN EXAMPLE OF A SPEECH THAT USES BOTH PERSUASIVE AND INFORMATIVE ELEMENTS

Good evening, everyone. I'm here today to talk to you about the importance of recycling.

First, let me give you some information about the impact of waste on our environment. Did you know that in the United States alone, we generate over 250 million tons of trash each year?

And much of that waste ends up in landfills, where it can take hundreds of years to decompose, releasing harmful gases and toxins into the air and water.

Now, I don't want to just inform you about this problem. I want to persuade you to take action.

Recycling is one of the easiest and most effective ways to reduce our waste and protect our planet. By recycling just one aluminum can, for example, we can save enough energy to power a TV for three hours.

So I urge you all to make a commitment to recycle more. Start by separating your recyclables from your trash and making sure they're properly disposed of. Encourage your friends and family to do the same. Together, we can make a real difference in the health of our planet.

Thank you for listening, and I hope you'll join me in taking action to protect our environment.

HERE'S AN EXAMPLE OF AN INFORMATIVE SPEECH ON HOW TO RECYCLE EFFECTIVELY

Good evening, everyone. Today, I'd like to share some information about how to recycle effectively.

Recycling is a simple and effective way to reduce our waste and protect the environment. But it's important to do it correctly in order to maximize its impact. Here are some tips to help you recycle more effectively:

Know what can and cannot be recycled. Different materials require different recycling methods, so it's important to know which items can be recycled and which cannot. Common items that can be recycled include paper, cardboard, glass, aluminum, and certain types of plastic.

Clean your recyclables. To ensure that your recyclables can be processed properly, it's important to clean them before recycling. Rinse out bottles and cans, remove any food residue, and flatten cardboard boxes to save space.

Use the right recycling bin. Make sure you're putting your recyclables in the correct bin. If your city has curbside recycling, you'll likely have a recycling bin that's separate from your regular trash bin.

If you live in an apartment complex or don't have curbside recycling, look for a recycling drop-off location in your area.

Educate yourself on local recycling policies. Recycling policies can vary from city to city, so it's important to educate yourself on what is and isn't allowed in your area. Check with your local recycling center or waste management facility for guidelines on what can be recycled in your community.

By following these tips, you can help ensure that your recyclables are being processed correctly and making a positive impact on the environment. So let's all do our part to recycle more effectively and protect our planet.

Thank you for listening.

HERE'S AN EXAMPLE OF A PERSUASIVE SPEECH ON WHY ONE SHOULD RECYCLE

Good evening, everyone. Today, I'm here to talk to you about the importance of recycling.

Recycling is one of the most effective ways to protect the environment and reduce our waste.

By recycling, we can conserve natural resources, reduce pollution, and save energy. But it's not just good for the planet—it's good for us too.

When we recycle, we're not only helping to reduce the amount of waste that ends up in landfills and oceans, but we're also conserving resources. Recycling conserves resources like water, minerals, and trees, and it reduces the need to extract and process new materials, which can be energy-intensive and polluting.

Additionally, recycling can help us save energy. By using recycled materials instead of virgin materials, we can reduce the amount of energy needed to produce new products. For example, it takes 95 percent less energy to recycle aluminum cans than to produce new ones.

But perhaps the most important reason to recycle is that it helps us build a more sustainable future. By recycling, we're reducing the impact of our waste on the environment and ensuring that future generations have access to the resources they need to thrive.

So I urge you all to make a commitment to recycle more. Start by separating your recyclables from your trash and making sure they're properly disposed of. Encourage your friends and family to do the same. Together, we can make a real difference in the health of our planet and create a more sustainable future for ourselves and generations to come.

Thank you for listening.

HERE'S AN EXAMPLE OF A SPEECH THAT COMBINES PERSUASIVE AND INFORMATIVE ELEMENTS IN AN EFFECTIVE FORMAT

Good evening, everyone. Today, I want to talk to you about the importance of recycling and how you can recycle more effectively.

Did you know that in the United States alone, we generate over 250 million tons of trash each year? And much of that waste ends up in landfills, where it can take hundreds of years to decompose, releasing harmful gases and toxins into the air and water. But by recycling, we can reduce the amount of waste that ends up in landfills, conserve natural resources, and save energy.

To recycle effectively, it's important to know what can and cannot be recycled. Common items that can be recycled include paper, cardboard, glass, aluminum, and certain types of plastic. But not all plastics are created equal, and some cannot be recycled in certain areas. Educating yourself on local recycling policies and guidelines is an important step in ensuring that you're recycling effectively.

Once you know what can be recycled, it's important to clean

your recyclables before recycling them. Rinse out bottles and cans, remove any food residue, and flatten cardboard boxes to save space. And make sure you're putting your recyclables in the correct bin. If your city has curbside recycling, you'll likely have a recycling bin that's separate from your regular trash bin.

If you live in an apartment complex or don't have curbside recycling, look for a recycling drop-off location in your area.

By following these tips, you can help ensure that your recyclables are being processed correctly and making a positive impact on the environment. But perhaps the most important reason to recycle is that it helps us build a more sustainable future. By reducing the impact of our waste on the environment, we can ensure that future generations have access to the resources they need to thrive.

So I urge you all to make a commitment to recycle more. Start by separating your recyclables from your trash and making sure they're properly disposed of. Encourage your friends and family to do the same. Together, we can make a real difference in the health of our planet and create a more sustainable future for ourselves and generations to come.

Thank you for listening.

The choice is yours. Are you going to make a *how* speech or a *why* speech? If you choose *how*, make sure you really are an expert on your subject. You should be giving 10–20 percent of what you know in any speech. And if you find you use everything in your mental library to speak on your topic, you probably aren't truly an expert. Resist the urge to fake it, and go learn more about your topic.

If, instead, you go with a *why* talk, avoid manipulation. Don't tell your audience what they should be thinking. Instead, tell them what *you* think, and see if the power of your perspective is enough to win them over to your way of thinking.

CHAPTER 13

WORDS, WORDS, WORDS

"A professional writer is an amateur who didn't quit."
—RICHARD BACH, AUTHOR

IF THE FEAR OF PUBLIC SPEAKING IS THE GREATEST OF all phobias, the fear of writing lurks near the top of that list. So many of us hate to write. Perhaps it was all the forced essays we suffered through in high school and college. Maybe it's because we hold bestselling authors in high regard and are shocked by how poor our writing is in comparison (speaking from personal experience here). Whatever the reason, most of us hate writing, especially those who must do so to earn a living (those poor souls know just how difficult the process is and they still need to wade into it, like tiptoeing into a shark-infested lagoon, hoping to get wet without getting bit).

We have some good news for you: you do not have to be a *New York Times* bestselling author to be an impactful speaker. Not even close.

First off, as we told you earlier, you're going to be remembered for how you left them feeling, not for what you said. The idea and the delivery (more on that later) are far more important than word choice. Our brains are wired to remember select bits of information (which is why we focused on it earlier), so all the extraneous vocabulary simply adds unnecessary embellishment—as the old Shakespearian expression goes, "gilding the lily." It's decoration and overembellishment for the sake of appearances. Puffery and clever phrases may impress some, but they do not help with understanding your message and main point; nor do they make the final speech memorable in the way you want. What good is remembering a one-off line and forgetting the point of the speech?

What's more, one writes speeches for the ears first. These are messages meant to be heard once and remembered. There is no review, no rereading of the transcript. One does not have to be Hemingway, Steinbeck, Faulkner, or Twain to make an impact.

Instead, focus on conversational language that is clearly understood. Formal language—such as that found in literature, print media, business publications, and the like—makes for terrible speeches. Talk *to* people, not *at* them.

Not only is conversational speech easier to understand and remember; it's also much, much easier to deliver. Polysyllabic SAT words are impressive in print. They are also quite challenging to articulate smoothly in a well-delivered speech. Make your job easier and more enjoyable by choosing language that is already comfortable for your tongue. Select words you would normally use. Your fifty-cent word, well delivered, is worth more than any five-dollar word that is tripped on and stammered out.

Keep your sentences short. Avoid long run-on sentences that can confuse listeners. Remember, the audience has only one shot to hear and understand you. They cannot check a transcript if you've confused them. Plus, if you use short sentences or phrasing, you can avoid gulping air. Periods allow you time to breathe.

Also, use active verbs and colorful language to paint a picture for your audience. Don't be afraid to excite others. You can hype messages you believe in. Related to this, please don't equivocate. We understand the need for accuracy and truth, and we know there may be people in the audience who will hold you accountable for any false claims you make. We're not suggesting you lie...ever. But don't sabotage your message either.

Let's say you feel passionately about childhood hunger, and you want to talk about it. You could couch your language in safe assumptions, like "Childhood hunger is one of the more serious concerns in our society" or "Childhood hunger affects many kids"... something banal. Sure, you would be on safe ground. No one could challenge you, and that's because you didn't really say anything. You avoided making a strong statement for fear of contradiction. Instead, be bold—"Childhood hunger is the most serious problem we face today" or "If we don't address childhood hunger now, we risk the collapse of our very way of life." Can you back up these claims strictly by fact? Probably not. In reality, no one can back up any opinion made in a speech after word-for-word factual analysis, primarily because you are making a statement of opinion mixed with fact. The numbers tell us there are a significant number of children not getting enough to eat. Our hearts tell us this is wrong, and your passion leads you to the opinion that the problem deserves more attention than others. If your intent is to truly help, don't get hung up on making strictly factual (boring and weak) statements. Put yourself out there. Be brave.

(While we're discussing writing and content, and keeping the above example of childhood hunger in mind, we would choose our phrasing to focus on one child...with a name. The story of one child, made personal and real for the audience, would be far more powerful than a broader story about a village with several nameless, anonymous children. It all goes back to connection through emotion. We, as caring people, would feel sadness for a faceless mob of children, but we'll certainly cry tears of anguish for the story of one child we know.)

Finally, Bach (from the opening quote) is right; the only thing separating you from a pro writer is determination. Step up, start writing your speech, and rewrite it until it feels authentic to you and you alone. You're not writing for a reader. You're writing for an audience of one—yourself—so you can deliver to an audience of many.

CHAPTER 14

MAY I HAVE YOUR ATTENTION, PLEASE?

WE LIVE IN A WORLD FILLED WITH ATTENTION DEFICIT, hyperactivity, distraction, and noise. It's a loud, clamoring mess out there. How are we ever going to get their attention?

That's an important question. You must win your audience's attention before you can effectively share anything with them. Attention is job one.

> **A STORY FROM GREG**
>
> Once, when I received an invitation to speak to graduates and their families at my high school, I had to consider how I would grab their attention and quickly establish a bond. Simply stating "I graduated from this school, just like you are about to" didn't suffice.
>
> Instead, I opted for something I knew everyone had done at least once. I began my speech with a quick game of Simon Says. This was

something we could share. It was familiar, but not excessively routine, making it memorable. I could integrate several of my speech points into the game, and I could turn the whole thing into an effective opening statement that got everyone's attention.

We did it to ourselves, this short attention span phenomenon. We've sped up the flow of information with rapid input from traditional and social media on multiple devices: phones, tablets, computers, TVs, digital assistants (Alexa, Google Home), and more. You can't escape it. It's in your home, your car, your workplace, and every public space.

All of this stimulation breeds short attention spans, and several studies have documented the effect. You, as the speaker, have no choice but to grab that short attention span and hold it as long as you can. You should break through the clutter.

Any journalist will tell you the process begins with a strong opening. (Side note: Psychologists say most people remember the beginning and ending of any sequence, whether it's a series of numbers or a presentation. Therefore, it's always important to start strong and end strong. Keep that in mind when you prepare content. More on that later.) In the news business, this strong opening is called a headline, and we know many people get their news strictly from scanning the provocatively written headlines instead of taking the time to read the entire article. For TV news journalists, it's called a lead (sometimes spelled lede). The opening statement is intended to captivate a distracted viewing audience engaged in various activities while tuning in the news.

Speakers sometimes call these headlines "banner statements," as they are used for setting up the theme and content of the ensuing talk in one interesting and concise line.

The strength of the headline/banner statement clearly correlates with the audience's engagement with the talk. Don't be shy; create the most evocative, interesting, and attention-getting line you can think of to begin your talk. Hook them from the start and you can keep them with you for as long as you like.

Within this process, your goal should be to build curiosity for your content without giving the whole thing away. Headlines and banner statements are teases. Get them listening and reserve some additional attention-grabbing material that you can sprinkle throughout the speech to keep them listening.

We have found that the pressure of the opening line can paralyze novice speakers. The pressure can leave them with a terrible case of writer's block.

Well, first off, as you've already read in this book, you should start at the end when creating your content—keeping your eyes on the prize of building the feeling you want those people to have when you are done. Given that, you shouldn't be writing your headline first. Create the rest of your talk content and find your strong opening later. That should take some of the pressure off.

If it doesn't, and you are still stressed about creating the right opening line to set up a successful speech, here are some options for you to consider:

- Ask a question related to your topic. This gets your audience thinking right away and, if the question is strong enough, builds the desired level of curiosity.
- Tell an anecdote or personal story. As you know by now, story is a powerful way to connect with people. We all love stories, and we really appreciate personal stories. If you share something meaningful to you, the audience will respond.
- Open with an interesting statistic or fact. We normally don't like to include too much formal data or numbers in our talks. "Numbers numb," as the saying goes. People zone out when the

information before them is better suited for a spreadsheet rather than a speech. Still, if you can find an interesting tidbit that sets up your content and puts it within an interesting context, go for it.
- Use a quote. You'll have noticed by now that we have liberally spread quotes from other writers and thinkers throughout this book. We're not shy about borrowing someone else's brilliance (with proper attribution, of course. You should never plagiarize someone's thoughts or work as your own…ever). T. S. Eliot, the great American poet, once wrote "Immature poets imitate; mature poets steal; bad poets deface what they take, and good poets make it into something better, or at least something different."[17] We're pretty sure he was kidding about the stealing part, but we're absolutely sure he gave us all permission to borrow great quotes (like we did, again, just now).
- Take a poll. This is akin to our suggestion of asking a question off the top, except, with a poll, you are soliciting answers from your audience. This makes the engagement process more active. Instead of letting them sit in the venue with their curiosity, you are instructing them to participate and get involved.

There truly is no wrong way to approach headline/banner statement writing as long as you are bold. Go big. Create a disruption. Get their attention.

---

[17] T. S. Eliot, *The Sacred Wood: Essays on Poetry and Criticism* (London: Methuen & Co., 1928), 125.

CHAPTER 15

THE ASK

START STRONG AND END STRONG. HOW DO YOU END A speech?

You end with "the ask," also called a "call to action."

If you are going to give a speech to a group of strangers, we assume you have a purpose in mind. You want those people to *do* something. You want them to change their thinking about something, support something, fight against something, contribute money toward something. We don't know what that "something" is, but you do. You have a reason to speak, and you are shortchanging your efforts if you don't clearly tell your audience what you want them to do.

This is difficult. Many people get queasy making the ask, so they don't. Or, at least, they don't do it effectively. Your ask needs to be strong.

That clarity begins with you. To help you distill exactly what you want from the experience, ask yourself the following questions:

- What *could happen* if the audience *does* as you suggest?
- What could possibly *not happen* if they *do* as you suggest?

- What *could happen* if the audience *doesn't do* as you suggest?
- What could possibly *not happen* if they *don't do* as you suggest?

When you can answer one or more of these questions to your own satisfaction and you can clearly and passionately explain the answers to an audience, then you are ready to make your ask.

This is you sharing a vision with your audience. You are painting a mental picture for them of what could happen if they follow your request or if they don't.

Yes, it's bold to ask people to trust you and commit their efforts and their resources to your vision of a better world. So consider this. You spent most of your speech, from the headline to the end, either informing them about something important or advocating for something absolutely vital. If you have done your job well, that audience will *want* you to spell out what's next. They want you to issue a call to action because you got them motivated, and that motivation needs an outlet. In fact, an engaged audience will be upset and disappointed if you do not make a clear ask at the end. They'll feel the preceding speech was a colossal waste of time.

Start strong and end strong. You owe it to the listener and your reason for speaking.

WAIT A SECOND. MAYBE TWO

The only thing more powerful than the words you use are the words you *don't* use. The absence of words…the pause.

Pauses are powerful, extremely useful, and totally necessary. Imagine walking out onto a stage with hundreds of people in the audience. They're applauding you, cheering, and clapping. You are already excited to be there to deliver your talk, and now the rousing reception is amping up your adrenaline. Now you're ready to explode. You just can't wait to talk, so you do, and no one hears the start of your talk. It's too loud. By the time the crowd realizes you've started and settles down to listen, they've missed the beginning. They feel confused and cheated out of part of your talk, and you feel unsure whether you should start over again or just press on. Either way, it's awkward. This is not a strong start.

Now imagine the same situation. You come out to your well-deserved applause. You look out onto the crowd and smile. You enjoy the welcome. You scan the room, looking at individuals, making eye contact before moving your gaze. Soon, the crowd noise lessens. It's just a smattering of hand claps now. And you keep looking, smiling, and not talking. It won't take but a second or two for the room to become absolutely quiet. Then, once it's completely quiet, you take one last look around the room and you notice that the audience, which is eager to hear what you have to say, is full of anticipation. They're on the edge of their seats, waiting for you to begin and give them what they came for. You take a breath in, and you begin.

That's how you start a speech. That's you in control of the room, making sure everyone is fully engaged and ready to go, especially you.

Pauses build curiosity, and you should feel free to pepper your talks with them. These silent moments not only encourage engagement by building anticipation, but they also provide needed breaks in the flow of information/messages coming from you at the podium. The audience uses these pauses to absorb and process what you have just told them. They don't need big chunks of time. We're not talking about building two-minute gaps in your speech. However, a few well-timed two- to three-second pauses can do wonders.

Again, it's a needed break for the audience and also for you. No one talks well for long periods of time without a quick break here and there. Speakers need breaks to wet their mouths, take in air, calm nerves, and keep on track.

The last two points are especially important. If you are a newer speaker, nerves may affect you. It's no big deal. Everyone has dealt with stage fright at some point. Pauses give you the opportunity to calm the anxiety before it gets to a point where it affects your speech. Keeping on track is also a huge pause benefit. Even when you've practiced a talk like you should, it's amazing how easily speakers can lose their train of thought. It doesn't take long before that lost feeling turns into worry and then panic. Not long after that, your speech can be unrecoverable.

Speakers are trained to think they have to speak all the time. Because of this, slight pauses feel huge to us. We worry that a second of silence is really thirty seconds—too long for the audience to ignore. They think, "I can't stop. They'll think I don't know what I'm talking about. I'll lose them just like I lost my place." But that's time distortion playing games with you. The audience doesn't mind if you take a few seconds to gather yourself and collect your thoughts. So go ahead. Stop when you need to. Take a breath. Look at your audience and see how they're responding to you so far. (That feedback you take from the audience during pauses is quite valuable. It helps you calibrate your talk to keep the listeners engaged.)

Pauses can also build drama and suspense in a talk. When you get to an element in your speech that you want the audience to either (a) be surprised by, (b) be shocked by, or (c) remember, don't forget to pause first as part of the setup for that line. The pause ensures the power line lands as it should, and you will create one of those memorable moments every speaker wants.

Incorporating pauses into your talk is essential for numerous reasons, with no valid reasons against it.

GET YOUR OKS

No, we're not talking about seeking approval. Once you have dedicated time and effort to create a speech that reflects your core message—what is in line with your life's purpose and values—it is your responsibility to assess, analyze, and ensure its accuracy. (You can also use this system before you craft your talk.) You need to ensure quality control.

Run your speech through the OKs system.

1. O—Have you clearly identified the **O**bjective of your speech? Can you summarize it?
2. K—**K**now you will make an impact. Do you have a way to measure and keep track of what you will ask of the audience? As management guru Peter Drucker says, "If you can't measure it, you can't manage it."
3. S—What's the **S**ignificance of what you're planning to say? What is the meaning, and does it have value for your audience?

Make sure you get the OKs before you take the stage.

THE SIX SS OF COMMUNICATIONS MASTERY

We've given you a lot of information to consider before making your next speech—especially if you are a true beginner. In our wish to be thorough and useful, we run the risk of overwhelming you, which is certainly not our intention. Therefore, inspired by the acronym above and hoping to distill this entire book into a memorable summary, we now offer you the six *S*s of communications mastery. Perhaps this list will help you remember other aspects of this book and recall them when you need them most.

- Self—know yourself. Know what you stand for and what you will fight against.
- Sound—your voice. Make the most of it as a tool and use it.
- Storytelling—the very soul of speeches. We communicate best through story.
- Structure—all speeches need it. Your audience needs it.
- Stage—learn how to use the space and how to move your body in that space.
- Spontaneity—develop the ability to change things up on the spot as needed. Flexibility helps us connect better with other people—our audience—in the moment. (Groups of people can be fickle. It's best not to adopt a set-in-stone plan but to react to what the audience sends back to you in real time.)

Professional speaking—using a stage and a microphone to make the biggest possible impact on your colleagues or community—is not a hobby or an occasional experience; it's a commitment.

PART 4

PUTTING IT ALL TOGETHER

CHAPTER 16

VOICE CARE AND MAINTENANCE

TIPS FOR THROAT CARE COME TO US FROM DANIEL TEADT, an opera vocalist and music professor at Carnegie Mellon University in Pittsburgh. He tells us, when you have phlegm (we know—it's gross), don't hack it up. The stress you put on your system will only create more phlegm. Instead, puff air out of your mouth or, if that doesn't work, close your mouth and *gently* clear your throat. Again, don't do a hard cough. Your vocal cords should not be engaged in this process.

Our mouths and throats need moisture to perform at optimal capacity. You may have seen or heard of speakers and singers sipping tea, and there are many people who swear by tea. We suggest decaffeinated. (Who needs the jitters when giving a speech?)

Water is best, and room temperature makes a difference. Also, it is wise to hydrate with water at least one hour *before* you speak. Remember, water goes down the esophagus, not the trachea.

For speaker prep, you want to avoid cold drinks. Cold is a natural constrictor. Therefore, if you drink cold liquids, you encourage your throat to close and compress. A closed throat does not produce your best voice.

What works best is warm or room temperature drinks. These provide you with the hydration (moisture) your system needs without the side effects.

You would also want to avoid milk, coffee, or any other drinks that leave a film in your mouth after swallowing. This often leads to one of two things: either you become distracted while trying to clean the residue out of your mouth with your tongue, which affects your speech, or you start making a smacking sound, a result of the sticky film working against your moving mouth. That is a very unpleasant sound for the listener. Know what else produces a mean coating in your mouth? Chocolate. Chocolate may be the worst thing to eat before a speech.

Sugary drinks—like juice—could cause you to salivate. Now you're calibrating your speech around swallowing as you work to keep your mouth from filling with saliva.

You have other opportunities to drink what you like. When you need to prepare for an important talk, keep your choices limited to room temperature water or decaffeinated tea.

While we're on the subject, smoking and excessive drinking damage a person's speaking voice. Some people find a "whiskey-cured voice" charming and appealing. Trust us when we tell you it doesn't take much at all before that tinge of smoker's voice becomes a grating, hard-on-the ears sound. Maintaining a top-notch voice means going easy on the booze and avoiding cigarettes altogether. Sorry if that ruins your fun. Sometimes excellence comes with sacrifice.

WARM-UPS ARE NOT ONLY FOR ATHLETES

The vocal cords are mucous membranes, not muscles. Still, they are susceptible to stress and need care.

And like muscles, it's important to warm up your vocal cords prior to extended use. The same thing goes for your mouth and tongue, both of which involve several muscles that can become exhausted if not used properly.

The thing is, it's very difficult to illustrate vocal warm-ups in a book.

Roger Love, the world's top voice coach, has several vocal exercises he uses with clients. We recommend you check out either of his websites—theperfectvoice.com or rogerlove.com—for more information. You can also search YouTube for Roger's vocal warm-up exercises.

Athletes, musicians, singers, and actors all warm up prior to performing. Speakers should too.

BREATH

"Breathing control gives man strength, vitality, inspiration and magic powers."

—ZHUANGZI, FOURTH-CENTURY BCE CHINESE PHILOSOPHER

Breathing is so foundational to life that its functions are found in our brain stems, where automatic functions of the body—like digestion, heart rate, and blood pressure—reside. Automatic. We do it always without thought. The average person takes some twenty-three thousand breaths a day while their minds are on other things.

If you really want to become a great speaker, you're going to have to think about breathing. It needs to become an intentional act that you control rather than an automatic function you ignore.

Breath powers your speech. Controlling it will ensure you speak at your optimal capacity. It is *the* most important consideration in speech making. It's that vital.

A STORY FROM VINCE

When I was the morning and noon anchor at WMUR-TV 9 in Manchester, New Hampshire, I got a call to visit a local elementary school between the two newscasts. This was a typical request, and I was always happy to oblige. The TV news game is all about attracting viewers...more eyes on your channel means more money from advertisers...which means job security (well, as much job security as you could have in that racket) and more money (theoretically, anyway).

This usually wasn't an issue. I could run out, do the event while the producers put the noon show together, and get back in enough time to review the scripts and get ready for the broadcast.

The only problem this day was traffic. There was a construction project that funneled extra cars and trucks onto the route I needed to get back to the station. I wasn't aware of this (it didn't make the morning news), so I found myself in bumper-to-bumper gridlock with the clock ticking to noon. This was also in the days before everyone had a cell phone. The station had a bank of cell phones crews would take with them when going out on stories, but I was only doing a school visit, so I never took a phone with me.

I had no way to contact the station to tell them I was running very late, my boss—the news director, who had been an anchor earlier in her career—suited up to take my place. I hurried back, left my car parked in front of the station, and ran into the newsroom with about five minutes to the start of the show.

My boss was in my chair, and that embarrassed me incredibly. I ran into the studio and told her I could go on. I had already dressed from doing the morning show, so all I had to do was clip on a mic. I figured

I knew most of the stories in the noon newscasts anyway. They were often rehashes of morning stories, so I could read the show "cold," as we used to say, without practice.

My boss relented (I don't think she wanted to go on anyway), and I took my seat as the show's opening graphics were rolling.

And it was terrible. The combination of panic and running around left me breathless, and I hoped I could catch my breath early on in the broadcast, except I didn't. In fact, as I struggled more, the problem got worse. It was not until the first commercial break that my breathing returned to something approaching normal—after the most important part of the newscast had already aired. Trust me, it was awful television. Easily the worst show I have ever done.

I rallied and got through the rest of the newscast. No one yelled at me after it was over. They understood, though I'm sure they were displeased about it.

That was twenty-three years ago. The memory haunts me to this day.

The quality of your breathing matters because not all breaths are created equal.

For speaking, you need to master diaphragmatic breathing.

Your diaphragm is a muscle found just under your lungs, which connects to the entire bottom of your rib cage. When you contract that muscle, it drops lower in your thoracic cavity and helps push your lower rib cage out, creating space that allows atmospheric pressure to fill your lungs with air. (Side note: You do not breathe air in; you let air in!) When you slowly relax the diaphragm, it moves up, closes your rib cage, and squeezes the air out of your lungs, which then leaves the body through the trachea (windpipe) and mouth and nose.

Why do you need to know this?

Because so many of us have developed poor breathing habits. We take shallow breaths while moving our chest and shoulders up during inhalation. Do you remember us telling you anything about head and shoulder movement during the breathing process? No, because those body parts moving should not be part of the process.

An imprecise understanding of the mechanics of breathing is to blame. Most of us believe we "suck" air into our lungs rather than allow the 2,116 pounds of pressure per square foot at sea level to fill the lungs. It is the opposite of what's really happening. Bad information leads to bad practices, which can cause bad performances.

Because the diaphragm rules the process, we need to focus our attention on that.

We all know from experience that insufficient air weakens your voice (see the story above). Knowing we need a good volume of air to speak well, we need to stop shallow breathing.

Instead, let your diaphragm tighten down into your pelvic base. You will know you're doing it right when your lower rib cage opens up and your belly and lower back expand. Now that you are breathing correctly—moving your belly instead of your shoulders and chest—you need to manage your breathing so you keep a reserve of air in your lungs. We suggest you breathe during the periods and commas of your speech. Aim to keep your lungs filled to about 60 percent capacity. This will give you the sustaining power you need for long talks without wasting effort on drawing in more air than necessary.

BREATHE WITHOUT DRYNESS

When discussing how the landscape will dry out after a rainstorm, meteorologists will tell you the wind, not the sun, does most of the work. Moving air removes moisture.

That's great for our soggy lawns and not so great for a speaker's throat and mouth. Dryness can ruin a speech as quickly as low air.

To stay hydrated, we suggest you drink water at least an hour before your speech. Taking sips of water at the podium will help you maintain your hydration, but it won't help much if you haven't already taken in water early enough to matter.

Then, to maintain that vital moisture, make sure you breathe in through the nose and out through your mouth. Nose breathing moistens the air as it comes through your vocal cords and into the lungs. And, as noted above, you don't want to be in a position where you have to snort in a lot of air at one time because your lungs are running low. That sounds terrible. Remember to "top off" your lungs through your nose and maintain a delicate balance between having enough air and not making unpleasant sounds.

WHY WE SHOULD NOSE BREATHE

Breathe through the nose when you are inhaling because it has a crucial benefit for speakers in improving speech and voice quality. ***Breathing through the nose can help maintain vocal cord lubrication, supporting better voice quality and speech.*** Of course, other benefits to consider include:

1. **Filtration:** The nasal hairs and mucus membrane in the nostrils act as natural filters, capturing dust, pollutants, and allergens from the air, which helps prevent them from reaching the lungs.
2. **Humidification:** The nasal passages add moisture to the air,

which helps to humidify it, making it easier and more comfortable for the lungs to absorb.
3. **Warming:** The nasal passages warm the air to near body temperature before it reaches the lungs, which can be especially useful in cold environments.
4. **Better Oxygen Transfer:** Nasal breathing leads to more efficient oxygen–carbon dioxide exchange in the lungs.
5. **Production of Nitric Oxide:** The sinuses produce nitric oxide (NO), a vital molecule in increasing circulation and delivering oxygen into the cells more efficiently. It also has antimicrobial properties, which can help combat harmful pathogens.
6. **Promotes Diaphragmatic Breathing:** Breathing through the nose can encourage deeper, diaphragmatic breathing, which is more efficient and healthier than shallow, chest-based breathing.
7. **Stimulation of the Parasympathetic Nervous System:** Nasal breathing can stimulate the body's "rest and digest" response, helping to reduce stress and promote calmness.
8. **Better for Oral Health:** Mouth breathing can lead to dry mouth, which can cause dental health issues. Breathing through the nose helps maintain a moist environment in the mouth, supporting oral health.
9. **Supports Proper Tongue Posture:** Nasal breathing promotes the correct resting position of the tongue against the palate, which can influence dental arch development, speech patterns, and overall facial structure.
10. **Reduced Snoring and Sleep Apnea:** For many people, nasal breathing can reduce the likelihood of snoring and the severity of obstructive sleep apnea.
11. **Enhanced Sense of Smell:** Breathing through the nose allows you to use your olfactory system better, providing a richer sensory experience with the environment.
12. **Protection against Respiratory Infections:** The nose produces

a mucus layer rich in immunoglobulins, which can help trap and neutralize harmful microorganisms.
13. **Elevated Cognitive Function:** Evidence suggests that nasal breathing can optimize brain function, especially during tasks requiring focus and attention.
14. **Regulation of Airflow:** The nose can regulate the volume and flow rate of the incoming air, which can be helpful during activities that require controlled breathing, like singing or practicing yoga.

As we listed above, there are numerous benefits to nasal breathing. Of course, there are situations where mouth breathing is necessary, especially during intense physical activity, or if you have nasal obstructions. For most of us, and most of the time, nasal breathing is helpful for your overall health, well-being, and communication.

GETTING CENTERED

Any yogi will tell you breathing properly reduces stress. Competitive athletes know this to be true. So do those serving in the military's Special Forces. Soldiers, sailors, and marines are trained to take a deep, cleansing breath before any big job. Snipers, for example, always take a centering breath before slowly pulling the trigger. If they don't take that moment to breathe and steady themselves, they could miss the shot and put others at risk. Our warriors have shown us that when calm and focus matter, breath matters.

Knowing this is powerful. If you happen to be in a venue, getting ready for an important speech, and your nerves are kicking in, this is an excellent time to stop and breathe. You'll be amazed by how well that works to restore calm and balance.

Proper breathing is a skill, and skills require dedicated practice for mastery. Here's a simple exercise you can do to improve your breathing.

Stand up straight and let your body be at ease. Open up for a deep four-count breath in through your nose and hold it in your lungs for seven counts. Then exhale through your mouth (like blowing out candles) over an eight count. Be still for a few seconds and then repeat. Pay attention to how your diaphragm and lower rib cage feel as you draw in a full breath. Feel your upper body relax as you release the breath. Soon, you will develop a new awareness of a process you have done all your life with little thought.

CHAPTER 17

MOVEMENT

"Body language is a very powerful tool. We had body language before we had speech, and apparently 80 percent of what you understand in a conversation is read through the body, not the words."

—DEBORAH BULL, ENGLISH DANCER AND FORMER CREATIVE DIRECTOR OF THE ROYAL OPERA HOUSE

PRO SPEAKERS MIX MOTION WITH WORDS. SOMETIMES people forget that speeches, though often confined to a small area of a stage, are really multisensory experiences. You listen to the words and the rhythms of the speaker's voice while you watch their expressions and movements. It all works together for one unified performance.

One helpful exercise if you are concerned about using your body on stage is to attempt delivering a talk *without speaking*. Use your body and facial movements to convey meaning. You will feel like you are playing an exaggerated game of charades. However, once you get comfortable with the idea, you will be surprised by how much you can say without saying a word.

You may also find this exercise becomes easier and more effective if you "inform" your body of the emotion you are attempting to relay in the nonverbal talk before you even begin. Decide up front if you are delivering a happy message versus a sad, angry, or frightened one. A variety of emotions await exploration, and you must find different ways to express feelings through movement, much like dancers do. (Reread the Deborah Bull quote above.)

Your body, remember, is an instrument. You will need to move it to get the best possible performance.

TAKING STOCK OF WHAT YOU HAVE TO WORK WITH

Before we get to how to stand and move and what to do with your hands (which everyone wonders), let's talk about the stage and what is on it for your use. These props are extensions of your body in that they are the physical, movable elements of the speech.

The first thing you'll have to sort out is podium or no podium. Personally, we don't enjoy using a podium. It's too confining. We like to move around, and the podium—to us, anyway—feels like a ball and chain around our ankles. Plus, we like nothing coming between us and the audience if we can help it.

We understand that some nervous speakers may seek refuge behind the podium. For them, it's a fig leaf to hide behind. Others may feel podiums give the festivities more gravitas. After all, the president of the United States speaks from behind a podium.

There is no right answer. Use a podium; don't use a podium. Do as you please. Only make sure the podium, if you use it, does not stifle your body movement on stage. You don't want to be stiff and still during your speech. That's boring to watch.

PowerPoint? If you must, go ahead and use it. Again, we are not in favor of it for our talks. It's a bit of a distraction and, in our video-obsessed culture, people can't take their eyes away from a lighted screen. If they're looking at the screen, they are not looking at the speaker's face. They're missing part of the performance, the intended experience, and perhaps part of the message.

If you have visual elements that add to your speech, or if you have data to present (make sure you keep numbers to a minimum—people want story, not data), then fine, use your slides.

And if you must use PowerPoint (or Prezi, or any other demonstration programs), please make sure you follow some simple rules. First, make sure each slide has an image. Text-only slides are mind-numbing and dull. Second, do your best to use seven words or fewer on each slide. Keep in mind that PowerPoint slides are not supposed to contain a full transcription of your speech. You should look at the audience, not the screen. (If you know your speech well enough, you won't need the slides.) As such, your deck should contain abbreviated summary points, in text, that are crucial for understanding your content. No long sentences. Don't even use sentence fragments if you can avoid it. Bullet points are great for PowerPoint as they force you to keep the text short and sweet.

Also, it is best to limit your fonts and font styles to two. That's it. Too much variety for variety's sake makes your presentation confusing. We use only one font with an option to "bold" any information that needs to stand out. This works.

We mentioned you should not use your slide deck as a teleprompter, feeding you the lines of the speech you should already have prepared and internalized. Notes, however, are fine. We don't feel you need to recite your speech "word perfectly" (meaning you accurately use every word you originally wrote for the talk). Good speakers use written text and often go off script when better phrasing comes to mind or if they are responding to how the room is receiving the message. We certainly understand that most speakers can't possibly memorize every line of a speech, especially if that speech will run ten, fifteen, or thirty minutes long. That's too much to memorize, and your audience knows that. They won't care if you occasionally reference your notes. When you do, make sure you lift your head and look back at the room *before* speaking—no one wants to stare at the top of your head while you're talking—and don't lift the notes high enough that they obscure your face. We want to see your face when you speak to us.

As for other visual aids, such as easels and props, all the rules above apply. Use them if—and only if—they benefit and help the audience understand your message. If your intent is to distract attention away from yourself because of a lack of confidence or nerves, don't do it. Take a breath and put yourself out there.

Now that we have all that sorted, let's talk about body movement.

BODY MOVEMENT
POSTURE

If you are sitting, make certain your feet are parallel and your hips, shoulders, and head are in balanced alignment. Sitting without alignment entangles your body and constricts your windpipe. You want unobstructed air to power your talk. When standing, stand up straight—no slouching—ankles, hips, shoulders, and head in balanced alignment. Keep your shoulders at ease, and do not let them creep up toward your ears. You should stand comfortably with your body as relaxed as possible and with your knees slightly bent. As you move, you may end up stretching, bending, or doing all kinds of movement in support of your story. It all starts with you standing up nice and straight.

As you stand, have your feet spread about shoulder width apart—parallel and not with your toes pointing in different directions—and put one foot behind the other. Lift the heel of your back foot a little. This "speaker's stance" is comfortable and allows you to move without appearing stiff.

We can't stress relaxation enough. Excess tension in the body will (a) affect your voice and (b) put stress on your body. Tension is a fear reaction. We relax when we feel safe and secure, as will your audience.

If you find it difficult to relax, remember to try this: Go to a quiet spot, and close your eyes. Focus on releasing all tension in your scalp. Then do the same for your forehead, then eyes and cheeks, then mouth and jaw, and so forth. Work your way down the body and remember to breathe deeply as you do it. Deep breaths help us get to a calm, relaxed state.

Believe it or not, relaxation on demand is a skill. It requires practice if one is to perfect it. So we recommend you do this exercise routinely. Do it at times when nothing is going on, and try it during stressful times. Teach your body to relax when you need it to.

Hands Part One

Hands are the bane of every speaker's existence. We all struggle with the question, What should I do with my hands? And the answer is whatever makes sense.

If you don't need to move your hands as part of your speech choreography, then keep them relaxed and down at your sides. Try not to fold them in front of you. This may sound picky and overly detailed, but from a psychological perspective, when you clasp your hands in front of you or fold your arms across your chest, you are closing your body language to others. It's a defensive posture, keeping others out of your space. Except you came to that room intending to welcome others into your world. That starts with maintaining an open posture.

You can—and should—use your hands to gesture and point as it serves your speech. Be mindful that too much hand movement will appear jittery. You'll need to calibrate how much is too much.

Rule of thumb: if the movement has a purpose, if it advances your story or message, do it. If not, don't.

Hands Part Two

This is a little advanced, so don't bother with all this until you feel you have comfortably mastered all the other elements of your speech. Ready?

You can use your hands—in fact, your entire body—to show the chronology of your story or talk. Pretty interesting, yes?

Here's how that works. Western first-world audiences (like those in the United States) are predisposed to see the left side of the stage as the start of a timeline and the right side of the stage as the end. Our brains are wired this way because we read from left to right in this culture.

When telling a story or anecdote where time is relevant, use your right hand (which is on the left for the audience) to gesture when speaking about events that happened earlier in time and the left hand (audience's right) to support material that happened later.

The same thing applies to your body. You could walk to the right side of the stage (again, audience's left) to begin a story and advance to the left (audience's right) as the timeline progresses. This is using hand and body movement to give additional context while verbalizing other information. Now you're creating that multisensory experience that audiences love. It helps them really engage with your content and lose themselves in what you have to say.

One quick note about this: make sure you reset your hands, or body, back to a neutral position when you are done talking through a particular chronology. It's a good nonverbal clue that you are moving on to other material.

Hands Part Three

Although it is generally better to maintain an open body posture toward your audience, there are instances where it is acceptable to place your hands in your pockets and step back from the audience. Let's say you are addressing a sensitive topic—such as child abuse or prostitution. This would be a time when you treat the audience gently and give them space to feel comfortable. These are times for quiet vulnerability, not boldness. Knowing when this type of movement is appropriate comes with experience and your growing ability to "read the room."

POINTING

Most Americans consider pointing rude. (Though, admittedly, our standards of rudeness have changed drastically in recent years. Have you noticed?) It's fine to point as long as the action is intentional and helps to amplify an element in your talk. If you need to point to people, consider doing so with an open hand versus one finger. Or use three fingers. This is something the Walt Disney Corporation trains its cast to do. The thinking is that pointing with three fingers comes across less rudely than using a single finger.

EYE CONTACT

In our culture, looking others in the eye when speaking to them is a sign of respect and courtesy. This is true if you are having a one-on-one conversation and the case when addressing a thousand people in a big event. You don't want to alienate people by ignoring them.

Look your audience members in the eye. If it's a large audience, you start by picking a person. Then, as you come to a natural break in the talk—a breath, a period, a new topic—you slide your gaze over to another person in another part of the crowd. You keep doing this throughout your speech. Try to make eye contact with as many people as possible without seeming manic. Don't jerk your head wildly trying to have a moment with everyone. In larger crowds, you are selecting representatives of the group with whom you have a connected moment.

Look people in the eyes, but don't stare. No one enjoys being started at. You're a stranger to your audience, and that will make your staring even more uncomfortable. Make eye contact with someone, hold it for a second or two, and then break it; move on to someone else.

WALKING

Yes, we are pro walking. We like when speakers move around on stage. It's even better if they can walk out among the audience. This movement creates interest and energy. Tony Robbins, the world-famous author, speaker, and coach, says "motion creates emotion," and he's right.[18] Movement will amp up your audience and give you energy as well.

As with all movements on the stage, it's always wise to be intentional. Walking without purpose is pacing. Don't pace. When you have a purpose in walking, like emphasizing an element of your talk, or asking an audience member a question, or illustrating something you are talking about, that movement can be magic. Again, it's all about creating an irresistible experience for the people who came to hear you.

---

18 "Are You Stuck?," *Tony Robbins* (blog), Mindset, TonyRobbins.com, accessed July 23, 2024, https://www.tonyrobbins.com/blog/are-you-stuck.

MIRRORING EMOTION

This can be subtle. Whenever you are talking about something that has an emotional component to it (let's say it's a happy memory about a favorite Christmas of your youth), but your body is not reflecting the emotion you are describing (in this case, your face is wearing a stern expression—you're frowning), those watching you get confused. Your body movements aren't matching the content they're hearing.

Be mindful that any emotions you are speaking to—directly or indirectly—need to be reflected in your physical person. That means facial expressions, posture, movement, even walking—all of it needs to be in sync. If you are talking about a frantic, hectic event while you're sauntering slowly across the stage, it makes no sense. You would never smile if someone told you about a person's death, yet we've seen people talk about death in a public setting with a smile or smirk on their face. Granted, those speakers were likely grinning as the result of nerves, but who cares? In the final analysis, all we know for sure is that the person is smiling while talking about tragedy. Something's wrong with them.

Emotional disconnect is jarring, so think about what your face and body are doing as you speak. If you find that difficult, make sure you practice your speech in front of a mirror. That way you can see what your movements are, and if they don't support the emotion of the moment, you can practice changing them to something more appropriate.

PERFORMANCE NOTES

We hope this next section comforts the nervous would-be speaker. This is permission—from us to you—to make mistakes in your well-planned talk. In fact, it's important that you do.

Human conversation is not perfect. The next time you are at a gathering, try listening in on some of the more animated conversations—the ones that seem to be keeping people's attention. If you listen critically, you'll notice whoever is speaking is not doing so perfectly. There's always some mistake in the monologue: a misspoken word, a stutter, an "um." If a person were to speak perfectly for a long period of time, they would seem robotic. They would seem "fake."

This happened to Hollywood voice coach Roger Love. Roger has worked with a very long list of A-list singers and actors. His website sizzle reel (https://rogerlove.com/) is loaded with clips from Keira Knightly, Bradley Cooper, Jeff Bridges, Reese Witherspoon, Gwen Stefani, and many, many more. Greg Smith, co-author of this book, is also a mentee and one of the Roger Love Method's Master Vocal Coaches.

One day, Roger got a gig for a video production, and being the pro that he is, he nailed it. Perhaps too well.

After watching the takes, the producers asked him to redo it all. The takes were all too perfect. (Roger has exceptional voice control and is one of the very few people on the planet who can sustain flawless voice control.) The complaint: it's "too perfect," so it's not believable.

So Roger reshot the gig in a "conversational" rather than scripted tone.

To be clear, we are not suggesting you build mistakes into your speeches. Roger is a unicorn. We all should aspire to his level of professionalism and near perfection. Audiences appreciate a talk that is smooth and professional.

The point here is "perfection" is unnecessary because normal people consider clean speech perfect. We're used to the occasional breaks that accompany regular conversation, and because that's what we're accustomed to, it's also what we like.

Audiences forgive small mistakes. It's normal. No big deal. Newer speakers sometimes freeze when they make a mistake because for them, in their minds, their tiny faux pas is enormous. They heard or felt it, so they assume everyone in the room is absolutely fixated on it.

In reality, if the tiny bumps in the speech aren't pointed out, your audience never even notices them. They are so small and insignificant, they don't even register on their radar.

Aim for clean and professional and forget about perfection. It doesn't really exist.

CHAPTER 18

VIDEO

"You're not anybody in America unless you're on TV. On TV is where we learn about who we really are. Because what's the point of doing anything worthwhile if nobody's watching? And if people are watching, it makes you a better person."

—MOVIE DIALOGUE, NICOLE KIDMAN AS SUZANNE STONE-MARETTO IN *TO DIE FOR*, 1995

WHEN WE WERE YOUNG, TELEVISION WAS THE KING OF media. It was the most powerful way of reaching the masses, and stars were born on that little screen.

TV still has its place of prominence (do you know anyone who doesn't have a TV set?), but it is no longer the big dog that sits on the porch alone. The internet, with an overwhelming assortment of vlogs, YouTube videos, web videos, and more, now competes very effectively with TV for the eyes and minds of America.

For this section, however, it's a distinction without a difference. Video is video. All the internet did was proliferate it and make it nearly omnipresent.

Let's spend some time making sure you're ready to be on camera, because the cameras are everywhere.

A STORY FROM VINCE

When I was a graduate journalism student at Emerson College in Boston, we had class assignments that were meant to mimic what we would do as actual reporters. Every morning, our class would split into teams of two, and those teams were assigned stories to cover in the city. We would take turns working as the other person's videographer. Each team would conduct field interviews, shoot cover video, and reporter stand-ups (the part of the final news story where you actually saw the reporter on camera. As ego-driven TV students, we loved stand-ups the most!). Once we were done shooting, we would rush back to school, write and narrate our stories, and edit them for the student newscast later that day. These were deadline-driven exercises, much like reporting is. The greatest story in the world is garbage if you file it too late to air. Because we were students, many of us (not me) would be a bit laissez-faire about deadlines, and our professor—Marsha, a seasoned news professional—would pounce on the tardy reporter in training in front of all of us, saying, "If you were in a real newsroom, you'd be fired, fired, fired!" Those of us who cared moved as quickly as we could to meet the deadlines.

Perhaps it was because we were working fast (or because we were such newbies who knew nothing yet) that when my friend Sharman and I went to cover a winter story, we weren't really prepared.

I don't remember the issue, but the story involved the underground garage for the Boston Common. In a city severely short on parking spaces, this facility was vitally important for tourists and commuters alike.

It was wintertime, so I was wearing a black wool overcoat. My L.L.Bean casual coat wasn't an option. I had to look professional for my stand-up.

Once more, winter paints a gray picture outside. Plus, we were in the underground garage, which is pretty dark to begin with. This became a nighttime shoot in the middle of the morning.

The other challenge was we didn't grab a tripod before leaving school. News photographers often shoot from their shoulders, and that's what we planned on doing. The problem was that I'm close to 6' 7" and Sharman couldn't have been over 5' 8".

So when it came time for Sharman to shoot my stand-up, she had to shoot at an up angle to capture my face. Also, in the low-light environment and with the black coat on, the final result looked like a ghost head floating in the night. Not flattering and not professional.

But we were on deadline, so we had no choice but to rush back and use it.

I wish I could tell you this was the last time unflattering video footage of me made the air, but, of course, it wasn't.

ANGLES

When you are on camera, you want to make sure your entire face is seen. This means both eyes are visible, no profile shots. Being shot from the side can make your features look more severe. Plus, it appears that you were caught in the moment rather than willingly participating in the exercise. Most good interviewers know how to position their cameras so most of your face remains in the shot.

As I allude to in the snippet above, you really want to avoid being shot on an up angle. It is never flattering. Up-angle shots deepen the circles under one's eyes and exaggerate double chins. You will look older, heavier, and tired in up-angle shots, so if you are the guest in a video interview situation, don't be afraid to ask for the camera to be at eye level.

While eye level is best, being shot from above is not bad as a plan B. Most people look younger and just plain better when shot on a down angle. If eye level isn't an option for some reason, choose to be shot from a downward angle rather than an upward angle.

HEADROOM

Tight spaces make people uncomfortable. It's true of the physical world and the video world. If a frame touches the top or side of your head while shooting, it looks weird. It also elicits feelings of claustrophobia from the viewer. They may not be aware of it top of mind, but their subconscious knows something is "off" about what they're seeing, and that distracts from the message. You want to be shot (or shoot others) with a little room at the top of the head and with room on the side. The general rule to follow if the subject is facing in a particular direction (sometimes you can't avoid partial profile shots) is to try and have two-thirds of the empty frame in front of their nose and the remaining one-third of the empty frame at the back of their head. We like seeing the person have room to look forward.

While on the subject of framing a shot, let's talk about distance to the camera. Many people are camera shy and prefer the thing as far away from them as possible. Most people think this is fine. After all, we have wireless microphones to pick up the sound and a zoom lens to make the subject look closer, so why not shoot from across the room? What's the difference?

First off, when you zoom in on a subject, you end up compressing the background of the shot. Sure, the subject is the most important element in the video frame, but you want the background to look natural and not weird, don't you?

Second, zoomed-in shots magnify camera movement. Handheld camera shots that are zoomed in look like earthquake footage. A tripod helps, though it's really tough to eliminate all movement. Wind, people walking around, big trucks rumbling by—they all produce slight movement of your environment that can be exaggerated thanks to the zoomed-in shot.

If people can tolerate it, you are better off zooming the camera all the way out and placing it closer to the subject. The result is a steady, nice-looking shot with a clear background. Perfect.

LIGHTS, CAMERA, ACTION. THERE'S A REASON "LIGHTS" ARE FIRST

Lighting is the bane of every video shot. Whether in a studio or on location, getting the lighting right is very difficult. That's why Hollywood production companies employ professionals who solely focus on lighting and why smaller operations without the budget for these specialized professionals face challenges.

We won't get into detail about lighting here because this is a book on public speaking, not video production. We can offer a few insights that may be helpful.

Professional lighting schemes, at the most basic level, consist of key, back, and fill lights. The key light is the light source directly in front of the subject. It's the primary light and the most important.

Back lights, sometimes known as "hair lights" because they give definition to the subject's hairstyle are behind the subject. These lights add depth of field to the shot and separate them from the background.

Lighting technicians usually position fill lights off to the sides and adjust their heights based on the desired effect.

These lights can be changed with either gel or dynamic color LEDs—to change the color of the lights, often to mimic natural light or to "warm" or "cool" the tone of the lights—and dampeners (referred to as "barn doors" in video studios) that block part of the light source.

Additionally, natural sunlight can be manipulated, using various production tools to either block or reflect its rays in relation to the subject.

Again, lighting is complex, so let us offer you some simple tips to consider on your next video engagement.

1. Never fight natural sunlight. There isn't an artificial light source yet that can match the intensity of the sun. Avoid shooting with your back to sunlight (including exterior windows that allow light into the room). The strong light will make the video super bright and make it hard to see you.
2. Keep even lighting on your face. You want to avoid "hot spots," or areas of intense brightness that can come with uneven lighting.
3. Use light to reduce shadows on your face, but don't worry about eliminating all shadows. Shadows are natural, plus they help define features in the shot's frame. Obviously, you want to avoid harsh shadows, the kinds that make you look like you're in the witness protection program. Some light shadows are fine.
4. Stay in your light. If the shot is for an interview of some sort, you will likely stand or sit in a particular spot. That makes lighting you easier. However, if you are moving around—inside or out— you risk moving in and out of the light. Be aware of the areas that are lighted for video. Ask the camera operator or producer if you are unsure. And then try to stay in those areas.

HD IS UNFORGIVING

You could make the argument that cameras are too good today. Even your better smartphone cameras shoot in high definition. More pixels mean more detail. You should be aware of this.

If you wear makeup—either generally or specifically for the purposes of this shoot—be aware that heavy makeup looks, well, like you're heavily made up. It can look overdone. Don't cake it on. Cover what you feel you must and leave it at that.

Oily skin can be a problem in HD. That unnatural shine makes a person look nervous and sweaty, even when they're not. A light coat of powder is out of the question. Use a regular tissue, not infused with lotion, and blot your forehead and nose (these are trouble spots). This will not keep you looking shine-free forever, but the effect can often last long enough to get you through your segment.

DRESS NOT TO IMPRESS

When Queen Elizabeth II was alive, people always saw her wearing bright, vivid colors. From her hat to her gloves and coat, the queen's outfits were always eye-catching for their unusual hues.

The queen had to stand out. Often in a crowd of hundreds or thousands of people, she wanted her people to find her in the multitudes. Most, if not all, of them had come to see her, after all, so the royal's colorful clothing was really a courtesy more than anything.

For the rest of us commoners, standing out visually can be problematic. We're not throwing cold water on artists and other creative and expressive souls. If you want to dress garishly, feel free. You make the world a less drab place.

Serious speakers have other concerns, specifically that their appearance detracts from their speech and their message. That's self-sabotage and unfortunate, especially considering all the work they put into crafting their speech.

Kenn Venit, a well-regarded TV news consultant, used to give the following advice to news anchors: "Dress like a congressman."

What he means is dress elegantly and professionally, and make your clothing choice unmemorable. You don't want people registering and remembering what you wore in your video. If they do, they were devoting some of their attention and brainpower to your outfit when it should have been on your message.

LITTLE THINGS LOOK BIG

There you are, dressed and made up to perfection and framed well. You are in good light and ready to record.

Now you have to forget some of the earlier notes about body movement.

Sorry, I don't mean to confuse you. The issue here is when you are on stage, live, in front of an audience, you need to move to deliver an effective speech. Movement is part of the process. And because you are some distance away from those you are speaking with, you will move in bigger ways so those in the back can see. This is all similar to how actors in a live play speak and sing loudly for the benefit of the audience.

Video reduces your world to a slight, very focused box. Eye, facial, head, and hand movements all become exaggerated in this video frame. This makes brief movements appear much bigger and more distracting.

In video, less is definitely more. You should aim to keep your head still, as excessive head movement turns you into a real-life bobblehead, and you should keep hand movement to a minimum so you don't look fidgety.

You don't have to be a statue. You'll need to move your eyes, smile, and nod. Simply be aware that a brief movement goes a long way. So be intentional. Move with purpose and do so wisely.

VIDEO IS RADIO TOO

Let's not forget that video shoots also require audio. Sound needs to accompany good visuals to get a nice, professional product. How you use the microphone will determine if the sound quality is pro level or not.

If the mic provided is a fixed microphone, meaning you don't wear it but either hold it in your hand or use it from a stand, you want to position your mouth about six inches away. The host or producer will let you know if their mic system works better with you closer to it. (We've been on shoots where we felt we were eating the microphone; that's what they wanted.)

Ideally, you should speak a little to the side of the mic, not directly into it, unless it has a windscreen. This is because hard consonant sounds—like *P*, *K*, and *T*—can "pop." Popping happens when the hard sound forces a burst of air into the mic. It's distortion.

By speaking to the side of the mic, the air burst passes by the head of the mic without the pop.

The same thing can happen to mics you wear (sometimes called lavalier mics). Depending on how loud a speaker you are, you can wear these mics further away from your mouth than six inches. The trick here is to not look down toward the mic when speaking. That could produce the popping sound. These mics are designed to pick up your voice from a spot on your chest, so just look up as you normally would.

Some novice microphone users are tempted to raise their voice. Somewhere in their minds, they feel this makes their sound easier to register. You don't need to yell. Mics are part of an audio/video production set that includes sound amplification. If you are too soft-spoken, someone on the production team will turn up your mic. This can even be done after the recording session is over. Speak normally. Trust the mics to do their job while you do yours. You'll sound a lot better.

This next point may seem obvious, yet it's surprising how many people ignore it. Be aware of competing noise when doing live or recorded video. People talking, traffic, even running furnaces and air conditioners can create unwanted noise. You may only have a faint awareness of that noise in the moment because most of us are conditioned to continue with our daily conversations despite background noise. The video's viewers, however, will be very aware of the unwanted sound. At best, it's a distraction. At worst, it will drown out part of what you say, and the viewer will be denied that part of your message. Make a "listening check" part of your pre-video production checklist.

With the advent of AI programs—such as Blackmagic Design Fairlight, which has filters that will both reduce background noise and correct vocal inconsistencies—you may have greater freedom to disregard competing background elements someday.

DO I LOOK AT YOU? OR…?

When more than one person is in the frame of a video shoot, it always leads to the question of "Where do you want me to look?" It's been our experience that nonprofessionals don't handle looking (staring) down the lens of a camera very well over an extended period of time. Professional on-air talent learns the subtle tricks needed to make this appear natural and not creepy.

It's fine if you are the one speaking and you want to reinforce a point by looking at "the audience" through the camera. In fact, that can be very effective.

However, for most of the time you are on camera with others, you will appear more natural and more comfortable if you turn your attention to the others. This helps you avoid "staring" at the viewer of the video. Keep in mind, from their perspective, if you are looking down the lens of the camera, you are looking right at them.

And looking at someone too long makes them feel weird. Obviously, avoid moving your gaze all around. It will appear as though there's a fly in the room that stole your attention, and the rest of us watching the playback will waste time looking for it too.

The other thing to keep in mind is that video is a "parasocial" activity. This is a term TV news producers use, and it means having people interact in video in ways that mirror real-life social interactions. Think about how you behave in a conversation with several people. You would look at all of them from time to time. It's considered polite; you don't want people to feel ignored. The problem here is if you "ignore" people who are on camera with you, the viewer will think you are being rude to them by ignoring them. It's better to include everyone in your attention.

So the answer to the question, "Where do I look?" is everywhere you normally would if you were in a group conversation.

The same holds true if you are one-on-one with another person, perhaps an interviewer. You can look at the camera here and there; otherwise, look at the person you are speaking to. It's basically polite behavior.

Now, if you are alone on camera, you have no choice but to address the camera more than you would in the other examples. You are the show.

Still, as we mentioned before, people watching your video will feel strange if you stare at them. We recommend you break that stare from time to time. Look down as if consulting your notes or take a glance to the side. These little eye-contact breaks mimic how we actually talk to other people. If you are in a conversation with one other person, you don't maintain constant eye contact, do you? By the way, these breaks don't only help the viewer; they'll make you more comfortable as well.

CHAPTER 19

AGAIN, PRACTICE

"Sweat more in practice, bleed less in war."
—SPARTAN WARRIOR CREDO

GREAT SPEAKERS ARE MADE THROUGH TRAINING, SKILL building, and practice. It's like losing weight. There's no magic pill or silver bullet. You need some combination of meal planning and exercise, and the weight will come off. Same thing here. It's all training and practice. There are no shortcuts.

The word "practice" may register in your mind as "repetition." We understand why you may link these words. For us, they are original concepts.

Deliberate practice—or purposeful practice—is what you want. This is the exact thing that will elevate your speaking skills to the professional level. You can find a comprehensive explanation of the concept in Anders Ericsson and Robert Pool's book *Peak: Secrets from the New Science of Expertise*. For now, here's the short version.

Ericsson and Pool say simple repetition alone does not lead to personal development or skill building. Doing the same thing over and over again simply gets you the same result. To quote Albert Einstein, "Insanity is doing the same thing over and over and expecting different results."

If you want results, Ericsson and Pool say you must actively engage in deliberate practice, where you set well-defined goals, focus your efforts with proper intensity—not casually—and include feedback for strategic adjustments in the process. All of it should stretch you beyond your comfort zone. Practice the actual skill you need to strengthen or the actual speech you plan to give. Working on ancillary concerns will only distract you from your goals and make the process unnecessarily longer.

Consistency compounds. The more you practice, the more easily your new skills will kick in, and you'll see the result in a great speech.

As a general rule, you need to be a speaker in training every day, even if you don't have any speeches in the foreseeable future. Great speakers read, question, write, and speak every day. Days off are for amateurs. The good news is you don't need to make your daily practice a big, laborious thing. Even fifteen minutes of focused practice will give you results. It's really about the consistency, not the time. And even the busiest among us have fifteen minutes somewhere in our days to devote to becoming better at something we love.

Bo Eason, former professional football player, now storytelling and stage expert who coaches high-performing individuals on how to be the best in their chosen fields, sums it all up this way: "It takes twenty years or more to become the best in the world at something if you intentionally plan sustained, deliberate practice and build effective mental representations." When Bo says "effective mental representations," he's talking about seeing yourself succeed and attaining your goals.

Despite taking the time to read this book, you may not want to be a world-class speaker. You may not feel it is the best use of your precious time right now. Or perhaps you want to be good but aren't feeling the drive to become great. That's fine. It's your life, and no one gets good at anything they need to be pushed into. Greatness is for the willing and the hardworking.

If, however, you see a future owning the stage and commanding an audience's attention, you have the tools to do it. All you need now is some deliberate practice time.

DO IT OUT LOUD

It's kind of unbelievable. There's a person who wants to be a speaker. They have things they want to say and a voice they've worked to improve. And when it comes time to practice their speech, they do it silently in their own head.

Words sound very different in your imagination versus spoken—by you—out loud. Speaking the words you plan to use in your speech is the only way to be sure those words actually work for your mouth. All of us have words we say well and others we tongue-trip on. Don't make the mistake of speaking your words for the first time in front of an audience. You may need to practice out loud.

We've heard some people protest this idea, saying they don't want to practice at full volume because they may bother others in their home. Or they are embarrassed by what others may think when hearing it. Know this: pro speakers don't have those objections. They practice at full volume wherever they can. They'll run their lines in the car, at home, anywhere and everywhere. You need to hear your own speech as a quality control measure. It's not a bad idea to record your practice session and listen to it. We guarantee you will end up changing your planned talk after you've heard it in your own voice.

MEMORIZATION

Brilliant speeches are delivered head up. The confident speaker looks out at their listeners and delivers. They make eye contact, move with purpose around the stage, and create a memory for all in attendance.

The ideal begs the question, "Do I have to memorize my script?"

We will answer with a question of our own: "Can you?"

If you have that type of memory, fantastic. You should commit your script to memory and focus on giving a stellar performance rather than reading your lines. Of course, that's the ideal.

Then comes the honest realization that most readers of this book are likely not trained actors. You, perhaps, don't have the ability (yet) to memorize a longer work, such as an important speech. Don't worry. You can still be an impactful speaker, even if you can't memorize lines.

You can do so in one of two ways.

First, you can use notes. There's nothing wrong with that. Make sure you practice with your notes in hand and push yourself to refer to those notes less and less in subsequent practice sessions.

If you have the opportunity, try practicing with your notes in the actual speech location. There is a learning dynamic that occurs when you study material in the space where you need to recall the same information, such as for an exam or, in our case, giving a speech. Psychologists refer to it as "contextual clues." When you practice your speech in the room where you're giving it, your mind will create links between the content and the things you see in the room. When it's time to deliver that speech, you'll be surprised at how much more naturally the words will seem to come to you. You will have developed clues within the context of that room, and those clues will aid your memory.

And remember, you still have your notes on top of that.

So that's the first solution. The second is recognizing that writing pages of specific verbiage, and then reciting those very same words as you've written them, is unnecessary. Who says you have to give your speech exactly as you've written it?

What if, instead, you take your speech, where you have carefully laid out all the content you want to cover, and make an outline of it? Then, when you are on the stage, you use the points in the outline to recall the content. If you don't use the exact wording you first came up with, so what? No one in the audience will know. They never saw the original script. Chances are you will either remember much of the phrasing anyway, because you rehearsed it enough, or you will probably come up with even better wording on the spot. It could happen. When you practice your talk, your brain is at work editing. That process does not stop when you are done rehearsing. Your brain knows you have a speech to give, and it's doing its job of looking for better ways of doing that speech. It's happening on a subconscious level while you are living your life and attending to other things.

On speech day, don't be surprised when your brain generates content and wording that you did not have in your first few drafts. It happens, and it's great when it does.

So, no, you don't need to memorize your speech verbatim if that is not in your skillset. Remember what you can, and trust your brain and your notes with the rest.

CHAPTER 20

STAGE FRIGHT

MINDSET IS CRUCIAL IN CONTROLLING WHAT WE KNOW as "stage fright." You need to ask yourself, "Is this really fear I'm feeling, or could it be something else? Something far more productive and interesting?" You can harness your energy from fear, anxiety, and anticipation and turn it all into excitement.

Our bodies react to fear and excitement the same way. The heart starts pounding, and we become more aware of our surroundings. We see, hear, smell, and feel things we were oblivious to just moments before, and our breathing becomes rapid and shallow. Excitement and fear are so similar that if someone were to observe you in the state described above with no background information for context, they probably wouldn't know which emotion you were feeling and which label to apply.

Consider the possibility that it doesn't matter.

Believe it or not, you get to label what you are feeling. Are you anxious or eager to get on the monstrously high and ridiculously fast roller coaster? It's probably a little bit of column A and column B, but you get to decide what your experience will be. You can label what you're feeling—excitement or fear. Your body will react much the same either way. All you're really changing is your mind.

Now, we know you may be thinking, "That's easy to say and harder to do." Respectfully, we disagree.

Mel Robbins is a lawyer, TV host, and motivational speaker with an incredible following. Her book *The 5 Second Rule* provides an excellent technique for overcoming this internal battle between fear and excitement.

Robbins calls the five-second rule the one rule everyone must follow to be as productive as they wish and get everything they want. Her premise is we all do the things we like to do automatically. So no need to manage that. It is the things we don't want to do that come between us and achievement. Robbins likens it to parenting. When you have kids, your job is to encourage your children to do the things they don't want to do but must do to learn, grow, and be healthy. And there are times when we have to "encourage" rather forcefully (kids can be stubborn). Robbins believes we need to parent ourselves if we want to do what we need to do but don't want to do.

So she developed the five-second rule, which goes something like this: from the moment you have a productive, goal-oriented idea, you have five seconds to act on it before the moment is lost. According to Robbins, if you don't do something with that idea quickly, your brain will kill the idea. Remember, you don't want to do it anyway. Maybe stepping outside your comfort zone, or fearing failure, or feeling overwhelmed with other tasks prevents you from taking action on it. Whatever the case, if you delay action on the good idea you had, your brain will talk you out of it. You will overthink it and give yourself an excuse to not move forward. You will stay where you started.

Instead, Robbins says you must take an action within that crucial five-second window. The examples she gives during a TED

Talk on the subject include: state your intentions out loud as a way of committing, physically walk in the direction of the action you thought to take, write down a plan for moving forward, schedule the steps needed to move forward, send yourself (or others) an email or text about the idea, and when your idea involves the participation of others, boldly ask that person or people for their involvement.[19]

By following Robbins's five-second rule regularly, you will not only move more of your ideas from thought to reality, but you will also develop positive habits that will make you more productive and successful in the future. As with anything, repeatedly doing something—even doing the things we simply don't want to do—gets easier with practice.

Practice works for the pros. Some say that legendary singers Bing Crosby, Barbra Streisand, and Bruce Springsteen were/are afraid to go on stage. Meryl Streep, Tom Hanks, and Reese Witherspoon reportedly all avoid seeing their own movies. Current country music superstar Chris Stapleton has talked about how he likes to look at his wife and bandmate, Morgane Stapleton, while he performs. Seeing her reassures him and gives him strength.

Yet, regardless of the fear or nervousness, they all have produced significant bodies of work, and all, with the exception of Crosby, who died in 1977, continue to perform today. They have all mastered their fears—perhaps even relabeling the feeling as excitement—and found methods to do what they momentarily did not want to do. They demonstrate that you can love and fear something at the same time.

We wish there were a quick cure for stage fright, and we know it can be a serious thing for some. There have been several studies done

---

[19] Mel Robbins, "How to Stop Screwing Yourself Over," filmed June 4, 2011, at TEDxSF in San Francisco, CA, TED video, 00:21:40, https://www.ted.com/talks/mel_robbins_how_to_stop_screwing_yourself_over/transcript?subtitle=en.

to determine how significant this phobia is, including a Chapman University research project that confirmed more than a quarter of all people fear public speaking. It was, in fact, a higher percentage than those who feared snakes, bugs, clowns, and death itself.

As for why this is, we came across a biologist named Glenn Croston and his book *The Real Story of Risk: Adventures in a Hazardous World*. Croston theorizes that our early ancestors were in constant danger. They lived close to nature, and a whole bunch of bigger, faster, and stronger predators were intent on eating them. As a means of survival, they gathered into communities. Together, they could warn each other at the first sign of trouble and fight together.[20]

Those who contributed, collaborated well with others, and brought value to the group were recognized and rewarded, much like we still see in today's society.[21]

Belonging in the group and having a secure place in it were literally lifesaving. Ostracism from the group, on the other hand, was deadly. As a result, individuals learned to avoid offending their community, and according to Croston, this is a taboo that endures today.[22] We've carried it with us and warped it to cover nonlethal activities like public speaking.[23]

Now, as funny as that seems when stated plainly, ask yourself if there is a better explanation for why some of us get so worked up about speaking before a group.

So, no, there is no fast-acting remedy. Overcoming thousands of years of ingrained instinct is no small feat. You have access to resources if you feel the need. Dr. Joan Rosenberg wrote a won-

---

20 Glenn Croston, *The Real Story of Risk: Adventures in a Hazardous World* (Amherst, NY: Prometheus Books, 2012), 23–29.

21 Croston, *The Real Story of Risk*, 12–13.

22 Croston, *The Real Story of Risk*, 213–215.

23 Croston, *The Real Story of Risk*, 234–236.

derful book on the subject called *Ease Your Anxiety: How to Gain Confidence, Emotional Strength and Inner Peace* that you will find helpful. There are also coaches who can assist you on a more direct and personal basis. We provide that service, as does our friend Jonathan Altfeld of the Mastery InSight Institute.

Making a few adjustments to your mindset can help ease your nerves. Focus on why you are speaking and what you hope to accomplish. Understand the truth: that audiences want their speakers to succeed. They are on your side, so much so that they often immediately forgive any small mistakes you make during your speech. (If you ask them about it afterward, they honestly couldn't tell you about it. They forget about those things so quickly. It's the message that endures.) You can also focus on the genuine fact that your willingness to get on stage (nerves and all) and share your insights and expertise is an act of giving. It is a loving, charitable, and honorable act worth momentary discomfort. You could remember that no matter how badly you botch the speech (you won't really, but we're talking worst-case scenario), you will survive. It's not like those ancient times when offending the group meant exile and death. Sure, it may feel bad for a while, but you will go on and live a productive life. So will your audience.

And if you still feel shaky, remember Mel Robbins's five-second rule, the very embodiment of the Nike slogan "Just do it." There is power in the ability to stop dithering and will yourself into doing.

FAREWELL

DEVELOPING EXCELLENCE IN PUBLIC SPEAKING IS A PROcess. There is no external resource on the planet that can substitute for the real-world experience of giving speeches. Notice we never spoke to your intention of giving the occasional speech or becoming a professional. We're speech snobs in the sense that excellence should be the goal for every speaking opportunity, big or small. If it's worth doing, it's worth doing right.

Getting there does not have to dominate your life. John Maxwell, whom we have referred to a few times already, says to get really good at public speaking, you need only devote 1 percent of your day to practice, a little over fourteen minutes. That's because it's not the time; it is the consistency. Short, regular practice with focus and energy will compound the effect. And even though we're telling you now it's going to work, you'll be surprised by how well and how fast it does. You'll see. In fact, if you can commit to this for a year, you will develop more public speaking skills than 95 percent of the people walking the earth today. You will become elite.

Be careful with feedback. We all want it, and we forget feedback comes in varying quality. Only take appraisals of your work from people who know what they're talking about and who have your best interests in mind. Please disregard everyone else.

Be mindful that the vast majority of people in the world want to be entertained *and* given a relevant, meaningful message. You'll need to avoid boring, preachy, and overly long talks. This doesn't mean you have to water down your message. You need only add a little sweetener to make it more palatable. Maxwell tells us you have to know what your audience came for and then give it to them.

And finally, have fun because speaking before others is exciting.

If you feel personal coaching is the next step necessary in your development as a speaker, we invite you to contact us at commandtheroombook.com. We are always happy to help another communicator.

ACKNOWLEDGMENTS

WE WOULD LIKE TO THANK A FEW PEOPLE WHO SUPported us through both our comms careers and the writing of this book.

From Greg—I want to thank the wonderful educators and professors at Boardman High School, Miami University, and the University of Nebraska/Gallup University for believing in me and encouraging me. This book is an extension of you changing my life so I could add value to the lives of others and, hopefully, change their lives for the better as well.

Thank you to my partner, Rachel, and my sons, Roman, Brad (and wife Ashley), Sky, and Reagan. Thank you for loving and believing in me. To my extended family and friends—a list too long to detail—you are the best. I thank you all for your continuing love and support.

From Vince—To the fine professors at Emerson and my dedicated colleagues of my TV news days—whom I won't name here for fear of unintentional omissions—you put me on this path. Your collective influence shaped my career. Granted, said career has been, at times, bumpy...but it has always been interesting. Thanks for that.

Thanks also to my wife, Laurie, and my sons, Lucas and Neil, for always supporting me, loving me, and believing in me. I am a blessed man.

www.ingramcontent.com/pod-product-compliance
Lightning Source LLC
Chambersburg PA
CBHW060524080526
44586CB00012B/609